PLAN YOUR YEAR

HOMESCHOOL PLANNING FOR PURPOSE AND PEACE

PAM BARNHILL

Published by

🐾 spotted dog press

For written permission, contact info@pambarnhill.com.

ISBN: 978-0-9997421-2-9 (paperback), 978-0-9997421-3-6 (epub)

Editor: Harmony Harkema

Publishing and Design Services: MartinPublishingServices.com

FOR OLIVIA, JOHN, AND THOMAS,
WHO TAUGHT ME TO BE
A BETTER TEACHER

TABLE OF CONTENTS

HOW TO USE THIS BOOK

This book is broken into distinct planning steps you can follow to plan your homeschool year. In each chapter, I lay out exactly how to go about creating your plan and provide encouragement, inspiration, and ideas. Most chapters also include one or two sidebar articles by either me or another seasoned homeschooler to give you additional information, insights, or just another way of doing things. Finally, each section contains action items. By completing each action item, you will create a plan for your homeschool year!

COMPANION PLANNING FORMS

I have included copies of all of the necessary forms throughout the book. You may feel free to make as many copies of these forms as you need for your own personal use.

For color downloads of the forms, plus a library of additional forms, calendars, and editable planning pages, you can purchase the Planning Forms Library Lifetime Access at planyouryearforms.com.

FOREWORD

Planning a homeschool year is a daunting task. I know moms who are thrilled at the prospect of planning for a new school year and others who dread it. Either way, everyone usually flounders and flails along the way.

My own methods of planning a school year have evolved as I've become more confident as a homeschooling mom. I've learned to start with the children in front of me (knowing where they are and where they need to go), to consider my own strengths and weaknesses, and to operate from a mindset of flexibility and freedom. I've also learned to lean heavily on other homeschooling moms during the spitballing stage getting feedback from like-minded friends is not something to take for granted. That's where Pam comes in.

Taking a big beautiful idea and making it actionable and packed with purpose is where Pam shines—she's the first one I go to when I need to hash out the nitty-gritty. Over the past nine years, I've had the distinct privilege of picking her brain at every stage of the planning process. The simple steps she breaks down in this book will move you from a hesitant and shaky, "I think maybe we should homeschool next year?" to an enthusiastic "Hey! We're going to homeschool next year!"

It may seem like an impossible task to teach multiple children at different age levels and plan an entire year's work for purpose and peace. I'm overwhelmed by the prospect of it every single year. The book in your hands and the planning pages at your disposal will give you the tools you need right now (and then again next year, and again the next) to prepare for a year of home education worth relishing, delighting in, and living with gusto.

You can do this, homeschool mama. You've already taken the best first step by picking up this book. Now let's hook arms and let Pam show us the way.

Sarah Mackenzie
Read Aloud Revival

THE PERSON IN FRONT OF YOU

My husband and I started toying with the idea of homeschooling long before our children were school-age. I taught public middle and high school for seven years and had become disillusioned with the state of the public school system, its emphasis on testing, overcrowding in the classroom, and the increase in student behavior problems.

Knowing you want to homeschool early on in your children's life is both a blessing and a curse. Yes, I had years to research and plan for the first day of kindergarten. I had years to obsess over the perfect method of instruction, the perfect curriculum, the perfect day.

As you can likely guess, my children did not fit neatly into my perfect homeschooling plans. They had their own ideas, their own agendas, their own developmental timetables. It was a struggle to get them to sit for long stretches and soak up my carefully constructed units. My oldest did not read easily. She hated math. My second child was either clamoring to be a part of what we were doing, needing my attention, or destroying another part of the house.

It didn't take me long to realize I had missed a vital part of the planning process. In considering my vision of the perfect homeschool day, I missed the fact that my children are not perfect and neither am I (though I'm pretty close). My perfect plan ignored the most important factor of all: the people in front of me.

Make no mistake, I am not advocating exclusively child-led learning. Planning is a triad: the plan, the child, and the mother. Why was I creating an expectation for myself to spend hours outside studying nature when I hated being outdoors? I hate the heat, the bugs, the possibility of snakes. Ick. I don't know a woodpecker from a warbler, and yet I felt guilty for not checking off my scheduled nature study box each week. The same goes for elaborate crafts, piles of cute printables, and morning calendar time. While these things work great for some homeschooling families (maybe even you!), they were simply not me.

My epiphany came when I decided I was no longer striving for the perfect homeschool plan. Instead, I would strive for the perfect plan *for us*: the plan I would actually implement, the plan that would work for my children. I threw out everything that wasn't working, shut out the noise from the homeschool "experts," and blocked out the voices from my public school past. I took a long, hard look at who we are, what we are willing to do, and the things we actually enjoy. Then I scheduled in those things, became a happier homeschool mom, and started to feel successful. Funny thing is, my children thrived as well.

Homeschool planning is a big subject for one little book. Most veteran homeschoolers have created their very own methods of planning that work best for their families. Who am I to come along and say that my way is the best way?

I'm not. In fact, my goal in writing this book is not to show you the one right way to plan, but instead to encourage you and give you ideas for making the plan and the process *your own*. No matter how you decide to plan your homeschool, I want you to break free from your old paradigms about education and the expectations placed on you by the state, your family, and that supermom in your homeschool group. Instead, I want you to approach planning your homeschool by looking first at what is right for your children, your family, and yourself as a teacher.

Success breeds success, and confidence brings even more confidence. A good plan will help you build those things, and a good plan begins with the people in front of you, both in the mirror and across the breakfast table. Let's get started!

CHAPTER 1

CAST A VISION

When I was a teacher, there were not enough classrooms in the high school where I taught. Every room was filled every period. Therefore, during my two planning periods, I spent many hours in the teacher workroom grading papers, preparing lessons, and listening to the older teachers lament the fact that they no longer got to teach what they loved. Instead they spent all of their time teaching to the FCAT exam. I was saddened to see so many people who were passionate about their subject and their students be throttled by the system to which they had given their lives. It had a huge impact on my decision to homeschool, though I didn't realize it at the time.

Has anyone ever asked you why you homeschool? If they did, could you tell them? I used to have problems with this. I would stumble over my words, not really sure how to explain my convictions, worried that the next thing out of my mouth would give offense (easy for anyone when you're discussing a touchy subject, and super easy for me).

Then, one day, I sat and recalled those days in the teacher workroom. I thought about all the things I wanted to give my kids through homeschooling. I took the time to contemplate and write about what I wanted their home education to do for them—the opportunities, the practices, the things we valued in our day-to-day. It was only after doing that—after casting a vision for what our days could look like and what was important to our family—that I began to be able to articulate why we were doing what we were doing.

While some folks are looking for a fight when they question your desire to homeschool, many are simply curious. You might be the only homeschooling parent they've met. The concept is completely foreign to older generations. Whether their motives are confrontation or curiosity, I have found that the best way to answer people's questions is to have a clear idea of the vision you have for your homeschool.

In addition to answering questions, a vision also serves multiple purposes in your homeschool. It acts as a compass for making your plans and a call to action when motivation lags. As we contemplate how we want our homeschools to look, the only thing that really matters is the kids in front of us. Are we doing what is right for them? How would we know? To know that, we need a homeschool vision statement.

WHAT IS A HOMESCHOOL VISION STATEMENT?

Let's start with what a vision is *not*. It is not a picture of the human you want your child to be in twenty years. That is beyond your control no matter how hard you try. And we never waste time creating a plan for things beyond our control. It will only frustrate us.

So what *is* a vision statement? It is a statement of intent. It is comprised of the things that are important in your homeschool. A vision is not about what the future results of your homeschool will be, a vision is about what the day-to-day atmosphere of your homeschool can look like.

I love this quote by Rosabeth Moss Kanter: "A vision is not just a picture of what could be; it is an appeal to our better selves, a call to become something more."

Homeschooling without a vision is kind of like wandering around in the dark with your hands tied behind your back and then being surprised when you stub your toe. Why? Homeschooling is hard, and when we humans find ourselves facing something difficult, we are easily distracted and head off in directions we never meant to go, taking the easier path. When we come up against something hard, we might try switching curricula mid-year or we might feel despair our kids are behind other kids and push too hard (which rarely works), or we might even consider putting our kids in school.

> *Homeschooling without a vision is kind of like wandering around in the dark with your hands tied behind your back and then being surprised when you stub your toe.*

If you know your "why" for homeschooling, though, and can articulate it, then you are better equipped to face tough times and answer critics—even the one who lives in your head.

There are a number of ways to go about writing your homeschool vision. I am going to present a few different ways you can do this. Don't stress—just choose the method that appeals most to you.

ONE VISION STATEMENT METHOD

Your vision statement is a manifesto of sorts about the education taking place in your home.

A helpful place to start is to look into the future. Ask yourself, *As my children graduate from my homeschool and leave my home, what kind of people do I want to see before me? What skills do I want them to be proficient at? What books do I want them to have read? What ideas do I want them to have been exposed to?*

Imagine that future young adult standing in front of you. Now sit down and make a list of what he has experienced and what he is capable of. Try to keep it general, about 10-15 items. This is a document you will review one or two times a year, but even then you will not want to slog through 100 bullet points. List only general ideas and skills, not specific booklists and benchmarks.

The longer vision statement is not something you are going to spring on the stranger who asks you why you homeschool, but it might be something you discuss over tea with a friend who is considering the homeschooling path for her own family and who questions you more deeply about your methods.

Some vision statement bullet point examples might be:

- We want our children to be able to comfortably and effectively communicate through spoken word and in various forms of writing from formal to informal.

- We want our children to have a relationship with the great works and thinkers of Western culture, including the literature and philosophy of ancient Greece and Rome and the doctors of the church.

- We want our children to have a working familiarity with the geography of the world around them and be able to identify major countries, landforms, and water features.

Your specific vision statements may look very different in content from the ones above, but they should be unique to your family and the kind of education your desire for your children. Don't forget to include practical, physical, and artistic (music, dance, visual arts) skills as well as academics.

Keep in mind that a vision is exactly that—something you see for the future and not a current reality. While your vision statement will give you purpose as you plan and work, it may not end up being completely true. The person in front of you ten years from now may have different plans or abilities than you imagined. That doesn't mean you avoid creating a vision, but it does mean we consider the person and his or her individuality. *The vision is the tool, not the master.*

THE OUTLOOK INVENTORY METHOD

Another way to create a vision is to use the Homeschool Outlook Inventory. I have included a copy of this at the end of this chapter.

Imagine your children twenty years from now, as they are thinking back on their homeschool years. Now write the answers to these questions.

1. What do you want them to say about their homeschool experience?

2. What do you want them to do as adults (what are their skills, loves, desires)? (Remember: This is not a list of their accomplishments of the past twenty years, but instead skills and loves you would *like* them to have.)

3. What do you want them to think about you as a homeschool mom?

4. How do you want them to feel about being homeschooled?

Once you have given some thought to these four questions and written down your answers, consider how you can work toward those results. The means you use to work toward what you want your kids to say in the inventory are the statements that make up your vision.

To help you craft these vision statements, you are going to ask yourself the following three questions about the responses you wrote:

- What actions do you need to take as a homeschooling mom?
- What subjects and activities do you need to include in your studies?
- What kind of atmosphere do you need to create in your home?

Then write two kinds of statements:

1. In our homeschool we strive to . . .

2. In our homeschool we refuse to . . .

Talk this over with your husband. If you have older kids, discuss it with them.

About those "refuse to" statements: I often use the negative phrase to check myself where I try to push too hard or be too strict—it mainly checks my tendencies and not my kids' tendencies.

If you don't end up with negative statements, that is OK—you do not need to have both. This is *your* vision.

Here are a few examples:

- In our homeschool we strive to share good stories and discussions together as a family every day.

- In our homeschool we refuse to be dictated to by man-made timelines, and we allow each student to work to his or her own potential and ability without being rushed or pushed by artificial constraints.

- In our homeschool we strive to practice basic skills like reading, math, and handwriting with consistency that will lead to mastery.

A series of these statements will comprise the vision that you have for your homeschool.

You can write as many of these statements as you need to in order to encapsulate the vision you have in mind for your homeschool, but the idea is to create a broad view of what you hope to accomplish. You should end up with ten or fewer statements or your vision will likely be too specific.

Here is an example of how one of my outlook inventory statements translated into a vision statement.

Under "What do you want them to say about their homeschool experience?" I wrote, "We got to do things I couldn't have done if I had gone to school. Those things we got to do enriched my life." I would love for my kids to describe homeschooling to someone that way one day.

So I wrote a vision statement that looks like this:

> "In our homeschool we refuse to let table-learning rob us of the opportunity to get out and experience the world. We will not value seat work over feet work. Homeschooling lends us an amazing opportunity to be in the world and learning from it. These opportunities will be seized."

I personally know this is a particular issue of *mine* because of my introversion and my public-school-teacher-mindset baggage. Therefore it is important that this is part of my vision as a reminder, so that when I am faced with the decision to attend a half-day gardening class for twelve weeks, participate in a cool field trip, or take off school for three weeks and travel across the country with my kids, I will remember that experiential learning is just as important as finishing the math book.

THE ELEVATOR PITCH

In business circles, a short one- or two-sentence synopsis of a business's purpose and benefits is called an elevator pitch. This pithy statement is the answer to the question, "So what do you do?" I have a homeschooling resources website called *Homeschool Solutions with Pam Barnhill*. When I meet someone and they want to know what I do, I tell them, "I have a website that provides helpful tips and resources to homeschooling moms."

> **"** *If you know your vision, then you are able to evaluate opportunities, curriculum, and plans against it.*

As homeschoolers, we can use the elevator pitch technique to create a one- to two-sentence vision statement for our homeschool. This is a great tool to have when strangers ask why we are homeschooling, but it is also a fabulous tool to have as you sit down to craft your homeschool plan each year. Why? It can become a litmus test for us as we plan. Test everything you are considering adding to your plan against the statement you make in your elevator pitch.

Let me give an example. Back to my website for a minute. Let's say I am approached by a company that sells barbecue sauce. They know my audience is largely moms, and they offer me compensation if I will post about their barbecue sauce on my blog. For a moment I might consider partnering with this brand. Yet if I held that barbecue sauce up to my elevator pitch, I would be able to see that even though I could possibly spin it to fit my content (kind of), it really doesn't fit with my vision of providing helpful tips and resources for homeschooling moms. So I say no to the sauce (darn it).

It is the same as we plan our homeschools. If you know your vision, then you are able to evaluate opportunities, curriculum, and plans against it. If it doesn't fit, toss it. You have a standard to evaluate against.

HOW TO USE A HOMESCHOOL VISION BOARD FOR INSPIRATION
by Amy Milcic

IT'S NICE TO HAVE OPTIONS. Different homeschools need different tools, resources, and routines.

And those tools, resources, and routines may change as your homeschool goes through various ages and stages. In an effort to best meet the needs of our homeschool, I had to change up our approach to a homeschool mission statement. The traditional list of rules and goals on a white piece of paper just wasn't cutting it. But I knew we still needed something to keep us on track. Something to reference when life gets busy or we're caught up in our learning adventures.

At the time, our homeschool consisted of five boys ages 12, 10, 6, 4, and 1, plus a squirrelly mom who tends to jump down more rabbit holes than Alice. We needed a simple and affordable solution that could benefit all of us.

WHAT IS A HOMESCHOOL VISION BOARD?

A homeschool vision board is a DIY visual tool that displays your goals, dreams, and themes for your upcoming year. It's a collaborative project; you work with your kids to discuss, select, and create your homeschool vision. I define a homeschool vision board as *a collage of images, quotes, art; all that inspires and encourages, combined to give an overall sense of a theme or topic.* A homeschool vision board is a visual representation of your homeschooling goals, hopes, and dreams for the upcoming year.

A homeschool vision board can help if you:

- Tend to over-plan your year
- Have good intentions but lose focus
- Have different ages and stages
- Have difficulty staying on track with goals

I'm a planner girl and love the planning process. All those books and resources and great ideas are exciting and energizing until it comes to following through. That's when lists and plans and piles start to stack up in my beloved planner. Brilliant ideas are forgotten on slips of paper and sticky notes. I always have the best intention of sorting through those ideas but find they evaporate when I need them the most. Jumping down rabbit holes with my boys is awesome, but I consistently need a way to get back on track.

As my boys get older, I find we're functioning with an erratic homeschool schedule. After fighting the chaos, I've learned to embrace what is and just roll with it. I need practical tools and resources to remind me of our purpose and goals. I'm a visual person (one of the reasons that I love all those planners and lists). If I can't see it, it usually doesn't happen. I need more than just words. My boys love visual reminders, too. Homeschool vision statements (a set of principles you select to guide and support your homeschool goals) are typically one of the first things you're encouraged to create when you begin your homeschool adventures. You "need" a vision statement, or your homeschool will fall into a pit of despair and ruin. And I have nothing against vision statements per se. They're helpful to many families. A traditional, written homeschool vision statement, however, does not work for us. When we tried to use a written homeschool vision statement, it sat in a binder and collected dust. In the middle of a busy homeschool day, I'd forget what it said, get completely off track, and struggle to regain focus.

After giving the whole situation some thought, I realized that our homeschool needed a *visual* reminder of our vision statement, something that's easy to see and reference throughout our day. A Homeschool Vision Board was the solution!

BENEFITS OF A HOMESCHOOL VISION BOARD

A homeschool vision board provides you with a visual reminder to reference throughout your day. When you place it in your homeschool area, you'll find it a helpful and inspirational resource to keep you on track. If you have younger kids in your homeschool, a homeschool vision board is fantastic because pre-readers and early readers can understand and benefit from the visual cues.

Your homeschool vision board can be a fun, collaborative project that's easy to put together. Using a few affordable items, as well as common household materials, you can work with your kids to find and create pictures to represent your homeschool goals, hopes, and dreams for the upcoming year. One of the best parts of a homeschool vision board is that every member contributes to its creation. It truly is a collaborative effort that unites your family and encourages ownership of your homeschool.

OUR HOMESCHOOL VISION BOARD

The beauty of a homeschool vision board is that it's a custom creation that represents *your* family's interests and goals. Every board will have a different look and feel that makes it unique. Our homeschool vision board has always been a work of collaboration. My boys and I have fantastic conversations about past homeschool years and what we're looking forward to in the year to come. We love listening to each others' ideas and figuring out ways to merge them to create a homeschool vision for all of us.

As you work on your homeschool vision board, you share thoughts and feelings about your homeschooling adventures. You find yourself looking forward to studying subjects, picking out volunteer projects, and planning field trips. The best part: your homeschool vision board becomes a collage of the good intentions and hopes of your entire homeschool!

All ages can participate in the creation of your homeschool vision board. Little ones can scribble on paper or point to pictures in a magazine (heck, they can even rip them out). Older students can work with younger siblings to plan and prepare. Pre-readers and early readers are part of the process, working beside older siblings. Everyone has a sense of ownership and feels recognized.

If you're looking for a creative, hands-on project that brings your family closer together, you'll want to gather your supplies to get started right away on your homeschool vision board!

For more information about how to create your own homeschool vision board including a free printable tutorial with questions, visit Amy's website at https://rockyourhomeschool.net/product/ create-your-own-homeschool-vision-board.

HOW TO USE YOUR VISION

Now that you have a printed copy of your vision in your workbook, keep it handy. I will be asking you to do a vision check often as you work on the various steps, and you might need to take it out and use it in your planning.

Every year, as you sit down to plan and evaluate curriculum, pull out your vision statement and reread it to refresh your memory. You may choose to make changes to it. As your children change, and as you change and grow, the vision should change and grow with you. Use it as a starting point for deciding what plans to make and what resources to buy. The following chapters will show you how.

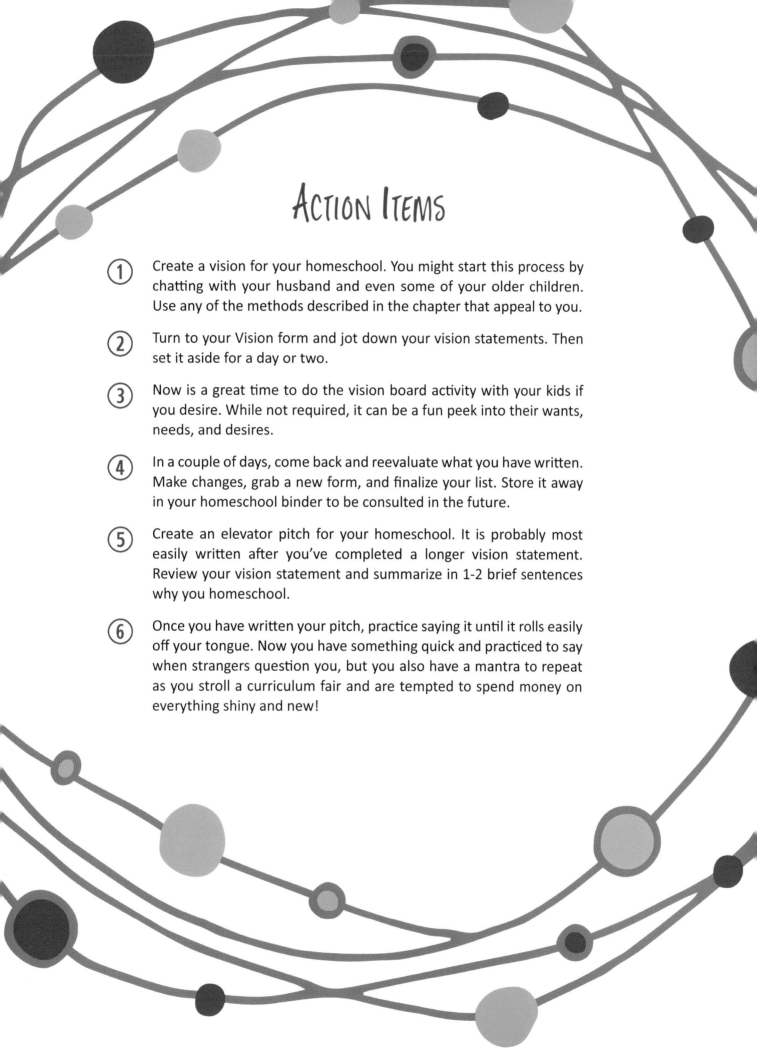

ACTION ITEMS

① Create a vision for your homeschool. You might start this process by chatting with your husband and even some of your older children. Use any of the methods described in the chapter that appeal to you.

② Turn to your Vision form and jot down your vision statements. Then set it aside for a day or two.

③ Now is a great time to do the vision board activity with your kids if you desire. While not required, it can be a fun peek into their wants, needs, and desires.

④ In a couple of days, come back and reevaluate what you have written. Make changes, grab a new form, and finalize your list. Store it away in your homeschool binder to be consulted in the future.

⑤ Create an elevator pitch for your homeschool. It is probably most easily written after you've completed a longer vision statement. Review your vision statement and summarize in 1-2 brief sentences why you homeschool.

⑥ Once you have written your pitch, practice saying it until it rolls easily off your tongue. Now you have something quick and practiced to say when strangers question you, but you also have a mantra to repeat as you stroll a curriculum fair and are tempted to spend money on everything shiny and new!

Outlook Inventory

What do you want them to say about their homeschool experience?`

What do you want them to do as adults (what are their skills, loves, desires)?

What do you want them to think about you as a homeschool mom?

How do you want them to feel about being homeschooled?

HOMESCHOOL VISION

_____

_____

_____

_____

_____

_____

_____

_____

_____

_____

_____

_____

_____

CHAPTER 2

CRAFT EFFECTIVE GOALS

I learned to write educational goals back when I was in college working on my teaching certificate. Educational goals are pretty easy to write. They all start with, "The student will," and end with some kind of measurable outcome. Here's an example: "The student will write a five-paragraph essay with an introduction, three body paragraphs, and a conclusion."

Pretty simple, right? The problem with this goal is that it's not clear what's important. Is the student communicating effectively? We don't know. What if the student wrote a brilliant essay that moved you to tears, yet had six paragraphs? Has the student met the goal?

Badly written goals are useless and can even be silly, but that doesn't mean all goals are bad. Goals can be a helpful tool to guide you and your student through a fruitful year of learning. Let's take a look at how to craft effective ones.

With homeschool planning, it is always good to start at the beginning. Before a single resource is purchased, before a single dollar is spent, I like to take a look at the person I will be teaching. What do I know about that person—my child? What are their strengths? What progress have they made over the past year (their successes)? What areas do they need to improve in, and how do I need to stretch them?

THE GOAL-WRITING PROCESS

Before we create goals. we are going to complete the following steps for each child:

- Identify what already works
- Identify strengths
- Identify areas to address

To do this, we are going to use the Goals Worksheet included at the end of this chapter.

FROM PAM'S PLAN

One curriculum product line that has always worked well for us is All About Reading and All About Spelling. My kids' language arts skills improve each year using these programs. And they love them.

Last year I thought that I needed a new language arts program. Why did I think that? I am not sure. My kids were making progress in this area where we had always struggled, but somehow I thought that moving to a new all-in-one program would be better. I was tempted by the shiny samples I saw online. (Yes, it even happens to me.)

So in March, I pulled out my credit card, spent about $200, and bought the new program. It was so teacher-intensive. The boys hated the reading selections, and I was constantly making substitutions. There were many moving parts, and it lacked the incremental approach that makes AAS so effective.

This is why it is important to make note of what is working well in your homeschool and why. I can't stress enough to write down what is working, and before you make any changes, look at those notes!

WHAT WORKS WELL

We are going start by taking a look at what has worked well for you in the past. If you are a new homeschooler, feel free to skip this section.

STRENGTHS

Take a look at your child's strengths. I encourage you to list the areas where your child excels and areas in which they made significant progress during the past year. This is important for a few reasons.

First, when a child has a strength in an area, that doesn't mean we can sit back and relax about that subject. Instead, it is an opportunity to play to that child's strength and provide additional enrichment.

Many times a child's area of strength is also an area of interest. When we are able, it is important to cultivate and allow them time to pursue those areas. It is good to remember areas of strength and interest as we plan so we can build in extra enrichment time.

Significant progress is also something to record. This will remind you what has worked this year and how hard work—yours and theirs—pays off.

One success I recorded was when we turned a corner in math with my daughter Olivia. Through trial and error, we finally found a math program with a method that works wonderfully for her. We now know that slow and steady progress and practice will bring understanding and mastery. I want to always remember that, just in case some shiny new math program tries to distract me, so I made sure to write it down.

AREAS FOR IMPROVEMENT

Next, consider those areas where a child needs significant improvement. This will remind you what subjects to allow extra time for this year and what skills to work on. Remember to think more broadly than just math and reading. While the main focus of our goals is academics, we are educating whole persons. So list areas of character or practical life skills that need to be developed as well.

Note: While our natural tendency will be to zero in on every little fault or weakness we would like to correct, limiting it to 3-5 areas on which to focus will make for a far more productive and sane year.

STUDENT INPUT

Another thing to consider is whether to include your older children in the goal-setting process. Ask them to tell you what they see as their strengths and weakness. The conversation may reveal why they have been struggling in their areas of weakness. You can also have them help you write their goals. This teaches valuable writing skills and gives them ownership of their education.

Give your child the opportunity to offer input into the course of study as well. It is not important whether a fifth grader studies chemistry or zoology for science, as long as they are studying science. Letting them choose will encourage them to work harder at a given subject because they are personally invested in the choice.

WRITING YOUR GOALS

Now we can begin setting goals. Goals provide a direction for the year and a framework from which we decide on subjects to study and purchases to make.

While the previous sections provide specific areas where a child needs enrichment or extra help, your goals will reflect the full scope of your homeschool year. So how should we go about setting goals?

GOALS SHOULD BE SPECIFIC AND MEASURABLE.

The first hallmark of a great goal is that you address a specific area and decide how you will determine your success.

> **Weak goal:** Olivia will learn to write.

> **Strong goal:** Olivia will write four days a week, focusing on outlining, research skills, summarizing, adding style, narrative form, and poetry.

At the end of the year, you can look at your record sheet and see if the second goal was met—the specific action can be measured with "Yes, we wrote four days a week, and we focused on the listed skills."

GOALS SHOULD FOCUS ON BEHAVIORS, NOT OUTCOMES.

Remember, we are starting with a person here. When it all comes down to it, we can't make them eat, sleep, or learn according to our desires or timetables. So I like to focus on what I can control—the behaviors and habits rather than the outcome.

Weak goal: Olivia will memorize the multiplication tables (12x12) by May 2020.

Strong goal: Olivia will spend 15 minutes a day, four days a week, practicing her multiplication facts using [resource of your choice].

The weak goal above is something you really have no control over, and in writing such a goal, you will possibly be setting up your child to fail. The strong goal is something you have complete control over, and it will possibly require some creativity on your part to make the process interesting. Which goal is more likely to lead to success? In my house, the weak goal would be stressful for everyone. On the other hand, we can rock that strong goal and have fun doing it.

GOALS SHOULD FOCUS ON LEARNING, NOT JUST COMPLETING.

This is why we homeschool, right? We want to focus on the whole person, ensuring they have an individualized learning experience.

> **Weak goal:** Olivia will complete Math-U-See Gamma by May 2020.

> **Strong goal:** Olivia will score at least 90% on each test in Math-U-See Gamma before moving on to the next chapter.

The first goal does not guarantee learning; it only guarantees that the box was checked. The second goal focuses on the mastery of the mathematical skills presented in the curriculum, as evaluated by the testing tool provided.

If Olivia has not mastered that material by May 2020, then the goal will continue the following year. The purpose is not to "complete the fourth grade book," but to master the material presented, no matter how long (or short) a time that takes.

Note: It is OK if you don't know what curriculum you will be using right now—we will get to that in Chapter 3. If you do, though, feel free to use that knowledge in making your goals as I have here.

GOALS, MASTERY, AND HIGH SCHOOL CREDIT

I think that learning for mastery applies even for high school—don't check the box if your child doesn't know it—but I know moms are anxious about the fact that they need to award credits for a transcript. To that end, you have a few options.

Option 1: If your high school child is not finished with all the work, they simply have to continue to work during the summer. They can decide if they want to work harder during the school year or school year-round.

Option 2: Consider that most public school students do not complete an entire text in a year and are still awarded credit. According to the Homeschool Legal Defense Association website, most curriculum developers consider completing 75% of the book equal to one credit, but that shouldn't simply mean leaving the end of the book undone.

You should plan to complete 75% of the book by assigning fewer questions and practice problems when appropriate or selectively skimming some topics. Maybe a documentary would be more appropriate in place of some chapters. Use common sense. If a math topic is a prerequisite for later mathematical study, don't shortchange it!

Option 3: You can also award a credit for hours worked even if a text is not complete. This will come in handy when you are using collected resources to design your own study instead of a single published text or curriculum.

GOAL-SETTING FOR MOMS
By Dawn Garrett

GOAL-SETTING IN YOUR HOMESCHOOL can be an eye-opening and school-enhancing experience. I had homeschooled my children for a number of years before I went through the process of setting goals for one of their upcoming school years. The process looked at their strengths and struggles, yes, but the activity revealed a great deal more. Drilling down into the struggles and looking for what needed shored up showed me where I had left out foundational pieces to give my kids a platform for success.

It wasn't just the process of writing their goals, though, that encouraged me to set goals for myself. When I wrote my vision for our homeschool, I saw much I could have wished for in my own education. I want to give this beautiful thing to my children, but I want pieces of it, too!

The process of goal-setting for moms is very similar to the one Pam outlines for our children. Print a form for yourself. Go through your strengths and weaknesses.

Some questions to ask:

- What are you really good at? What's going very well in your homeschool? What are you most confident in teaching? What practices do you love? What makes your days go well? How do you best embody your homeschool vision?

- What could use some more support? Where are the holes that need patching? What are you least confident to teach? What practices do you wish you were doing? What makes your day challenging? What parts of your homeschool vision need to be emphasized?

- Which of the children's goals needs to be prioritized as your goal? What scheduling or logistical issues can be supported by your goals for the year?

Sometimes other eyes can help round out perceptions. I've noticed that I (and most moms, I think) tend to focus on weaknesses; I'm always very aware of failings but am less quick to acknowledge what goes well. When I worked in an office, we had a 360-degree review process. Our management, peers, and any direct reports gave input toward the annual review. As I thought about that practice, I determined that it would be very helpful to ask my children and my husband what they see as strengths and weaknesses in our homeschool. Asking for input from others helps to broaden, balance, and clarify perceptions.

After this, I pray about all of the information I've gathered. Where does the Lord want me to focus my attention? What do I need to learn? How can I best help my children? I like to let the process sit for a day or two here. I want the cream to rise to the top. It's important to prioritize and be really sure which areas I want to focus on, and the subconscious does good work. I know that I can really focus on, at most, five things (and three is better). Because I'm responsible for helping establish and achieve the goals for my children, keeping fewer homeschool mom goals is helpful.

Finally, I return to the goal sheet and finalize the specifics of what I want to work on. By drawing from our vision, my kids' goals, and the goal sheet, I have all I need to identify those 3-5 goals. I try to choose one, at least, from the strengths column. I put a high priority on any scheduling or logistical goals. The final selection(s) are the most important improvements to make from the inventory.

Writing goals is a helpful exercise when you're thinking through planning your school year, but their real power is found in taking steps toward achieving the goals. If you never review the goals and assess the growth, the whole exercise is meaningless.

I put my finalized goal sheet in my teacher binder and try to review it on Fridays and during the week between our terms. You may choose different timing; I think at the end of the month would work really well. You may find that you've achieved some of your goals and want to replace them. Because you've already done the work, you have an inventory to draw on and can add the next most pressing item from the list.

Writing homeschool mom goals can enhance your homeschool by helping you to be a better teacher. It forces you to think through what you are doing to set a firm foundation for your children, ways to enhance their learning experience, how to improve the logistics of your schooling, and your own growth as a learner and educator.

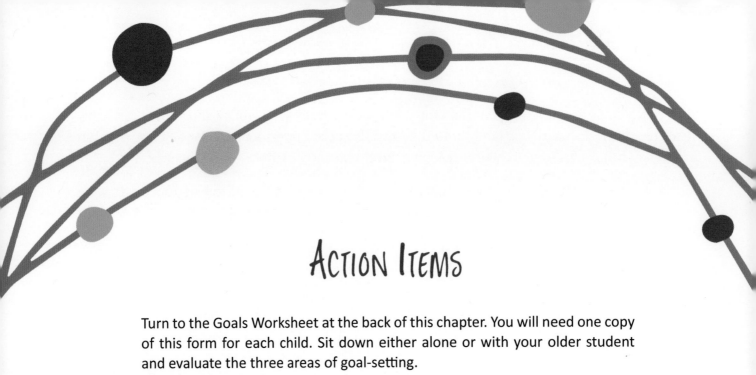

ACTION ITEMS

Turn to the Goals Worksheet at the back of this chapter. You will need one copy of this form for each child. Sit down either alone or with your older student and evaluate the three areas of goal-setting.

① First list your child's strengths and weaknesses.

② Next, outline the areas you would like your child to work on in the coming year.

③ Using the principles of goal-writing outlined in this chapter, write three to five goals for your child for this school year.

④ Repeat for your other children.

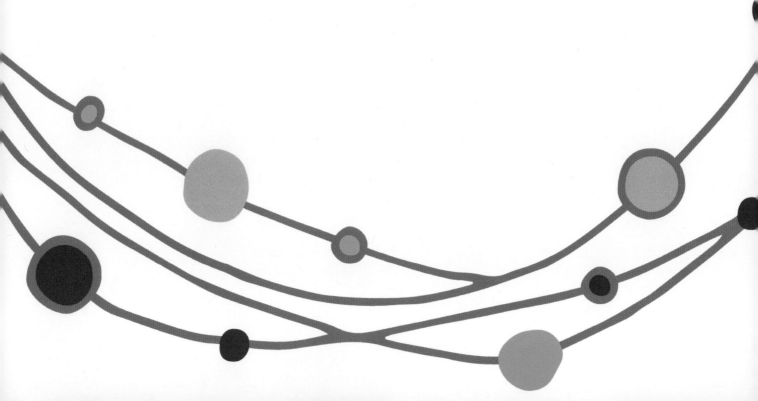

Goals Worksheet

Student:_____   Year:_____

WHAT WORKS	
STRENGTHS	
TO IMPROVE	

Student Goals

Student:_____   Year:_____

_____

_____

_____

_____

_____

_____

_____

_____

_____

_____

_____

_____

_____

CHAPTER 3

DETERMINE A COURSE OF STUDY AND PURCHASE RESOURCES

I confess I'm a bit of a knowledge junkie. My shelves are full of great books. I love museums of any kind. When I travel, I want to go and see the sights, not lie around by the pool. The world is filled with things to learn and there's so little time to learn them!

This is the crux of coming to a place of peace about homeschool planning. There is no way you have enough time to cover everything there is to learn. There will always be gaps in your child's education. My friend Sarah Mackenzie says to look at those gaps as gifts you are giving your child—think of all the things they will still get to learn when they are grown.

Learning does not stop at age 18. We don't close the book and say, "There, that's done." Once you make peace with this, planning a course of study is infinitely less stressful, and even fun!

WHAT IS A COURSE OF STUDY?

Very simply, a course of study is a list of the subjects you will study with each child and with your family as a group during a given year. You are determining what each child needs and how often he or she needs to work on each subject. Traditionally, schoolchildren study subjects like math, spelling, handwriting, science, reading, and social studies. Homeschool students need those subjects too. In addition, as homeschoolers we have the freedom to branch out and spend our time studying any other number of other wonderful subjects—which can be overwhelming, I admit. So let's walk through the process of deciding what to study this year.

WHAT ARE YOUR INFLUENCES?

Thinking about what to include on your list of must-dos this year will be influenced by four things. For some of you, all four of these factors will weigh into your course of study decisions. For others, it will only be one or two. Let's look at the big picture planning stage of choosing our resources.

VISION AND GOALS

This is where we get to use that vision for the first time. Have a look at it again, and see if it points you towards particular areas to focus on in your homeschool.

METHOD

Another factor that might determine what you will study in your homeschool could be your faithfulness to a specific method of homeschooling. If you are a proponent of classical education, you may decide to study Latin or a four-year history cycle. A unit study homeschooler is going to choose specific units that everyone in the family will complete together. Someone who does school at home will have a grade-level text for students to complete. None of these are right or wrong, but your method is something that will guide your path.

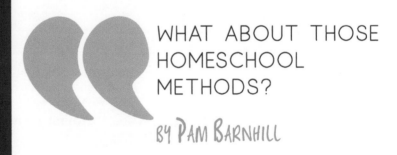

WHAT ABOUT THOSE HOMESCHOOL METHODS?

BY PAM BARNHILL

WHEN I STARTED MY RESEARCH ON HOMESCHOOLING, I fully anticipated recreating at home the same education I taught to my students as a teacher in a public school—the same education using the same methods I had received myself as a public school student.

Instead, I was amazed to discover that there are multiple educational philosophies and methods. They never mentioned those at all in teacher college. So what we have here is the good: you as a homeschooling mom have a number of different choices of philosophies and methods to use in educating your kids. We also have the bad: there is a *huge* amount of information out there to wade through before you can make an intelligent decision about which method to use.

My job here is to narrow down the information for you, objectively (I hope) present the pros and cons of each method, and then provide you with additional resources you can use for more information on methods you would like to study in depth. I experimented with every method on this list before I chose the path my family is now on. While I am not an expert in *following* any of these methods, I do consider myself an expert in *researching* them. It is with this expertise that I take you by the hand and guide you through the vast array.

1. UNIT STUDIES

HALLMARKS OF THE METHOD

- All students in a family are taught together using a unifying theme. That theme may be topical like the moon, the Civil War, or a specific virtue like attentiveness.

- When children are close in age, unit studies might be built around a single book or piece of literature like *Little House on the Prairie* or *The Very Hungry Caterpillar*.

- Families may complete one long unit study each year or multiple smaller ones.

- Typically, all subjects except math are taught through the unit study activities. The subjects covered are language arts, science, music, poetry, arts and crafts, history, geography, and Bible. A unit study might also include a detailed math section.

TOUTED BENEFITS

- The entire family learns subjects together, making planning and the daily schedule easier for mom.

- Units are often chosen based on student interests and therefore more likely to spark a love of learning.

- Subjects are integrated mimicking real-life situations and problem-solving. Life is approached as a whole instead of by isolated subjects.

MISUNDERSTANDINGS AND PERCEIVED DRAWBACKS

- Susan Wise Bauer argues that sometimes unit study families do not differentiate between skill and content subjects in a unit study. She contends that children "need organized, systematic grammar, spelling, and writing programs so that these important skills can become easy," and a fragmented teaching approach to these subjects will lead to gaps in the skill areas. She also argues that subjects like math and science have their own internal logic and should be studied separately.

- Charlotte Mason educators argue that unit studies make connections for the student and get in the way of the student making his or her own connections.

BOOKS AND CURRICULA

- Five in a Row: Volume 1
- Unit Studies Made Easy
- Konos Character Curriculum – Volume 1 with Lesson Plans (Volume 1)
- Units Studies from Homeschoolshare.com

WEBSITES AND BLOGS

- Unit Studies Page on The Homeschool Mom
- Five in a Row
- Cathy Duffy's Unit Study Index
- Homeschool Share Blog
- Blog She Wrote
- SusanEvans.org

2. CHARLOTTE MASON

HALLMARKS OF THE METHOD

- The Charlotte Mason method is named after its founder, who lived in England from 1842-1923. Mason was a forward-thinking educator who believed all children, regardless of rank or economic status, deserved and were capable of a broad liberal arts education.
- She started a teacher training college and parents' union to train school teachers, governesses, and parents in her philosophy and methods. She also outlined her 20 principles, which evolved over the course of her lifetime, in her six-volume set of books on education. It is recommended that those new to Charlotte Mason begin with Volume 6 of her works.
- The method is based on Mason's 20 Principles. A thorough understanding of these principles is necessary to understanding the entirety of Mason's philosophy.
- Simply following a set curriculum or booklist will not ensure a Charlotte Mason education without a grounding in the principles and her six volumes.
- This book-rich education centers upon the selection of high-quality, worthy (living) books, reading small portions of the book at a time, then having the children narrate what was read.
- Students under grade four do all of their narrations orally, while written narrations are introduced and phased in for all subjects at grades four and above.

- Mason focuses heavily on the training of habits. In fact, training good habits in children—such as attention, obedience, diligence, and more—make up a full one-third of a child's education. (The "Education is a discipline" portion of Mason's parent motto.)
- Other common practices within the Charlotte Mason method include spending a large amount of time outside, nature journaling, composer study, and picture study. The goal of a Charlotte Mason education is to spread a wide feast of the liberal arts before the student.

TOUTED BENEFITS

- Narration is a higher form of synthesis of information than simply answering a set of predetermined questions. Children's skills in listening, attention, speaking, and writing are all strengthened through narration.

- Students build good education and personal habits that are then used throughout life to continue their own education.

- Students are exposed to a feast of ideas instead of dry facts.

MISUNDERSTANDINGS AND PERCEIVED DRAWBACKS

- The Charlotte Mason method is sometimes perceived as a relaxed, child-led, or gentle form of homeschooling. Method purists feel this misunderstanding stems from people reading *about* the method from a second party instead of going straight to the source—Charlotte Mason's six volumes.

- Some homeschoolers feel that to faithfully follow Charlotte Mason, you must read the same books she read in her own schools, all of which are over 100 years old. Others argue Mason was constantly tweaking her own book selections from year-to-year and would have continued to consider modern books (of value) if she were alive today.

BOOKS AND CURRICULA

- Towards a Philosophy of Education: Charlotte Mason Volume VI
- Start Here: A Journey Through Charlotte Mason's 20 Principles
- For the Children's Sake
- Consider This

WEBSITES AND BLOGS

- Simply Charlotte Mason
- Ambleside Online
- Afterthoughts
- Joyous Lessons
- Charlotte Mason in Community
- Crossing the Brandywine

3. SCHOOL-AT-HOME (SCHOOL-IN-A-BOX)

HALLMARKS OF THE METHOD

- School-at-home looks just like the public school methods many of us were raised with. There are textbooks for each subject, often all from one publisher, and students sit and work through assignments in each book until the book is complete. Sometimes DVD or computer instruction is used to supplement or replace texts.

- School-at-home is often employed by families who do not have a problem with the methods of instruction in public schools, only the content or the environment.

TOUTED BENEFITS

- It is easiest to do what you know. For many parents, simply replicating school in the home or using a complete boxed curriculum adds a layer of ease to homeschooling that makes it doable.

- Traditional coursework makes creating a traditional transcript (and subsequently college admissions) a simpler process.

MISUNDERSTANDINGS AND PERCEIVED DRAWBACKS

- Many parents remember school and textbook learning as drudgery or remember their school experience as memorize, regurgitate, and forget. They want to offer what they feel is a more effective alternative for their children.

BOOKS AND CURRICULA

- Homeschool.com

WEBSITES AND BLOGS

- Meghan Carver, Lawyer Mom
- Starry Sky Ranch
- Minnesota Mom
- Prairie Lily Arts

4. CLASSICAL

HALLMARKS OF THE METHOD

- There are currently two types of education currently labeled classical: neoclassical and the liberal arts tradition. While both are strong on language and seek to return to a more historically-based curriculum, the approaches emphasize different aspects.

- Neoclassical education focuses on the three stages of the trivium as outlined by Dorothy Sayers in *The Lost Tools of Learning*. The grammar, or youngest stage, focuses on learning knowledge through memorization and skills through practice. The dialectic (roughly middle school) stage focuses on learning to reason through logic and questioning. Finally, the rhetoric stage, about the time of high school, focuses on applying the knowledge and logic from the previous two stages to write and speak with ability and authority.

- The classical liberal arts tradition differs slightly from the neoclassical in that the focus is on seeking the True, Good, and Beautiful through a study of good and great books, effective communication through speaking and writing, Latin, and formation of the moral imagination through story and myth.

TOUTED BENEFITS

- The aim of classical education is not to create a worker for a specific job, but instead a virtuous person who seeks to continue learning throughout his or her life.

- The focus on skills of communication—strong reading, writing, and speaking—make classically educated students well-rounded learners defined by their abilities instead of their job skills. The classically educated student has learned to learn and is able to adapt to change and obtain new skills easily.

- The ability to reason and craft an eloquent argument aids all areas of life from personal to public.

MISUNDERSTANDINGS AND PERCEIVED DRAWBACKS

- Some parents feel that a focus on rote memorization is akin to boring "drill and kill" and counter to critical thinking.

- Critics argue that the Eurocentric focus of classical education is elitist and excludes non-Western cultures.

- Classical education is seen as too rigorous by some, while others feel it downplays science and mathematics and the current trend towards an emphasis on STEM classes.

BOOKS AND CURRICULA

- An Introduction to Classical Education
- The Core
- A Guide to Teaching Classically
- The Liberal Arts Tradition
- The Well-Trained Mind

WEBSITES AND BLOGS

- Scholé Sisters
- Simply Convivial
- Expanding Wisdom
- Mt. Hope Chronicles
- Sandbox to Socrates

5. UNSCHOOLING

HALLMARKS OF THE METHOD

- All learning is child-centered and child-chosen. Students choose which topics they would like to study and the method they use to study them.

- There is no formal curriculum. If a student does not wish to study math and would instead like to spend all of their time reading *Little House* books, watching TV, or studying painting with watercolors, that is OK.

TOUTED BENEFITS

- Because students choose their own course of study, they are interested in what they are learning and therefore will retain the information.

- Students are respected as persons and not forced or coerced to learn against their will.

MISUNDERSTANDINGS AND PERCEIVED DRAWBACKS

- Arguments include that students will be ill-prepared for higher education or the workplace because they have not learned the necessary skills if they have not chosen to learn them.

- The lack of a consistent curriculum can cause huge gaps in knowledge and learning.

- Unschooling is often associated with unparenting.

BOOKS AND CURRICULA

- Teach Your Own: The John Holt Book of Homeschooling
- A Little Way of Homeschooling
- Moving a Puddle
- Free to Learn: Why Unleashing the Instinct to Play Will Make Our Children Happier, More Self-Reliant, and Better Students for Life

WEBSITES AND BLOGS

- Sue Elvis Writes
- These Temporary Tents
- I'm Unschooled. Yes, I Can Write
- Unschooling.org
- Journey Into Unschooling (invite-only blog)

There are other educational methods, many of which—literature-based, eclectic, etc.—are a hybrid of the above. If you are new to homeschooling, you might be wondering how important it is for you to choose a method of homeschooling immediately. My answer: it is not important in the slightest. Don't get bogged down in choosing a method and doing it the "right" way. Instead, rely on the *vision* you've created for your homeschool to get you started. There will be time in later years to read more about the methods that interest you and begin applying some of the principles from those methods to the education you design for your children. It isn't that methods aren't important, but any kind of consistent educational practice can help children learn. Don't get so hung up on the perfect method that schooling does not get done in your home. You aren't going to ruin kids by starting with one method and later switching to another. Pinky promise.

STATE REQUIREMENTS

While for most of us there are very few state requirements for homeschooling, a few states do have stricter guidelines. If you live in one of these states, you will need to consult your state requirements before making your choices.

PREPARED CURRICULUM

The third factor that will determine your course of study is a curriculum choice. While many parents, like me, are eclectic in their choices, some homeschoolers have decided to adhere to a particular curriculum like Sonlight, Ambleside Online, or Memoria Press. If you have a curriculum you use and love, then great! Your work in this area will be much easier.

Often in homeschooling circles. we use the word *curriculum* interchangeably for the word *resource*. (I do this myself all the time.) Curriculum, though, is a path of study laid out for the learner, not simply a single level or resource. A curriculum, like Memoria Press, includes a scope that goes beyond one year of learning and encompasses the whole of an education. Since this module is about choosing resources, if you use a prepared curriculum, that curriculum will influence the resources you choose.

I do not use curriculum—I choose resources and build my own path. Either way is perfectly valid.

If you are following a prepared curriculum, your work may now simply include using the resources in that curriculum to fill out your course of study worksheet and begin shopping. You may also want to tweak a few things and make some substitutions, or your curriculum may offer options you need to decide between. Also, be sure to verify that the curriculum is going to help your student meet all of his or her goals this year. You may want to consider any needed deviations or additions you're going to make in order to match your goals.

If you need to do any of this, or if your curriculum isn't prepared for you, let's move to the next section.

SKILL SUBJECTS VERSUS CONTENT SUBJECTS

An important distinction to make between homeschooling subjects is skill subjects versus content area subjects.

SKILL SUBJECTS

Skill subjects are those subjects that help a child to learn and demonstrate learning. Skills include things like reading, handwriting, composition, mathematics, and spelling. These subjects usually build on previous practice, and students should be able to complete these subjects while working at their own pace. Skills should be practiced often and to mastery. Most students will work on math every single year, while handwriting instruction will only be given until the student is able to write fluently and legibly (we hope). These subjects are important and should be done often because they are the basis for future learning for your child.

I have provided a list of considerations as a sidebar in this chapter to help you make decisions about these subjects. You do not need to follow all the considerations, but they might help you think a little more outside the box when it comes to education and what is "required."

CONSIDERATIONS FOR SKILL SUBJECTS
BY PAM BARNHILL

THE FOLLOWING SUGGESTIONS ARE MEANT TO inspire contemplation in you, the homeschool parent. They should cause you to question long-held beliefs you might have about learning and specific subjects in general. They are only meant to cause you to think, though; you should base your final decisions about how you will study a subject on your own research and convictions.

MATHEMATICS

- Do math regularly to keep concepts and procedures fresh.

- Memorize math facts to free working memory to do harder computations. If your child still struggles with math facts after a good effort at trying to memorize them, and you suspect a memory issue, move on to higher concepts but provide a chart of facts to use as a reference. Repeated use of the chart will aid in the memorization process. (A calculator won't be as effective at this.)

- If you have a child who previously knew facts but has forgotten them due to an extended break (summer), taking time to review the facts (we took two months once) is often helpful before moving on.

- Don't view math facts as a punishment you inflict on your child but instead, as a gift, you are giving them to help make the rest of their lives easier (kind of like the gift of long-lived teeth they get from good brushing habits). There is much you can do to make it fun, but don't cheat them of this gift.

- Kids grade two and younger can play at math to learn most of the needed concepts.

- Don't be afraid to skip ahead to a chapter in the math book on measurement or telling time if your child gets bogged down in a mathematical process. Often a break or change of pace is what they need. You can go back to the concept that was giving them problems in a week or so.

- Do not hesitate to sit beside kids as they work, scribing for them, using a whiteboard, moving manipulatives, and demonstrating procedures until they grasp the concept. I have found that some tougher concepts take a few days of demonstrating for kids to figure out how to do it independently.

- If you often find yourself only able to offer a single method of working a problem, and it doesn't work for your child, research alternate methods or consider a tutor or online class.

I knew my kids needed a math tutor when my only recourse was to explain long division more slowly each time they were confused.

- There is no particular magic to spiral or mastery math. Choose a math curriculum you and your child like to do and stick with it.

- Pay attention. Math is something that needs to be graded often. A child shouldn't move on to a new concept if they haven't grasped the last one. Computer programs don't always give a clear picture of success. If your child makes 85% on every test but misses the same two or three concepts each time, there is a gap that needs to be addressed.

READING

- Practice reading in short lessons daily.

- Once a child is reading fluently, stop reading instruction. Simply have them read instead.

- Let a child do their free reading a little below their current reading level to build fluency. They should read aloud to you at level and you should read books above level to them. This doesn't require a special test. Use a simple "just right" formula to determine which category a book fits into.

- Reading aloud is a different skill than reading to self. Have your child practice both, especially until he or she can read aloud well and expressively.

- If a child can talk to you intelligently about a book you have both read, then reading comprehension exercises are not necessary. Have informal conversations about books instead of assigning worksheets or book reports. Avoid accelerated reader programs that reduce the joy of reading to points to be earned.

HANDWRITING

- Children may need a boot camp after a break where mom sits next to them while they form all of their letters to correct errors that have cropped up.

- Once good, legible handwriting is established, stop handwriting instruction.

- Cursive handwriting might be easier for some kids to learn from the beginning. Cursive eliminates letter reversals and other issues that come from the print style of writing. (I wish I had done it!)

SPELLING

- Once good spelling is achieved (or if your child does not struggle with spelling) you can stop spelling instruction.

- Have your child keep a list of words that they commonly misspell from their own writing. They can practice spelling those words about once a week. Words should drop off the list as they master them.

- Developmentally, it takes a number of years before a child can transfer correct spelling from their spelling list to using it in their own writing. Some words they will use correctly early while others will take years, even though they can spell the words on a test. It's normal. Just point it out, have them add the word(s) to their frequently misspelled word list, and move on.

WRITING

- Children under age ten can narrate orally, and/or you can scribe for them. They can do copywork and dictation. They don't have to have a formal composition program.

- Consider that it is easier to write about things you know. When you ask young kids to imagine they are something and write about it, you are giving them a hard task indeed. They have no idea what it feels like to be a fish.

- Provide good models and rewrite those instead of having kids imagine their own stories. This allows them to practice writing skills on good material without the pressure of original thought. Writing includes a number of skills, from the physical act to having a thought to being able to hold that thought in your brain long enough to get it on paper. Break down those skills and practice them by doing handwriting, dictation, and narration before you ask a child to do all three skills at once.

- Kids need help with writing well into their teen years. You will not do your child a disservice by offering to write with them, providing guidance, ideas, suggestions for word choices, etc. This models good writing for your kid. It is a valuable part of the learning process and not "cheating."

CONTENT SUBJECTS

Content subjects are subjects like science, history, science, grammar, foreign language, and literature. These subjects provide depth and information to an education, but they are not vital skills.

So what does this distinction mean for your homeschool plan? Practice skills consistently and often. You have much more leeway in how content subjects are studied. For content subjects, you can combine students of different ages easily, follow their interests, even not do subjects every year (or at all). Unless your state has specific requirements for these subjects, you have total freedom in how you study them.

Do not be held captive by standard K-12 school practices. There is nothing that says specific subjects have to be studied in specific years.

While your kids are young:

- You can do the historical period or science topic of your choosing each year.
- You can skip science one year altogether and dig deeper into history.
- You can skip history one year!
- You can skip both for a term because you have a new baby.

 *Do not be held captive by standard K-12 school practices.*

Use the freedom that homeschooling offers you to create a custom learning experience that serves your family. This is why we created that vision. Really! It's OK.

Of course, once you reach the high school years, it probably isn't a good idea to study American History all four years. Then, you will need a little more diversity.

EVALUATE AND PURCHASE RESOURCES

I remember my very first homeschool curriculum fair. I entered the curriculum vendor hall giddy with excitement. I had been warned that I would be overwhelmed by the volume of choices available there, but in truth, I was not. Instead, I was delighted at the number of options and goodies to explore. I left that hall about $500 poorer and ready to get off my feet but happily anticipating the year to come.

I'm going to go ahead and admit that I severely over-purchased that year. Many of those resources we didn't really need and honestly never used much. They quickly made their way to the resale pile and (hopefully) went on to bless some other family. Homeschool resources is a multi-million dollar business with the marketing machine to match. It is incredibly easy to get caught up in the shiny, the new, the latest-greatest-problem-solving solution, only to end up poorer and frustrated by your choices.

I am happy to report that I no longer frivolously purchase items we don't need or use (well, not much). I have greatly improved at being mindful about what I purchase. This is partially through trial and error and partially through a great deal of self-reflection. While there are many factors that enter into finding just the right resources, here are the three I use to help me with my purchasing decisions.

KNOW THYSELF

I am not going to claim to be a frugal homeschool shopper. I strive to not be a wasteful one, but I still have a pretty decent homeschool budget each year, and I usually spend most of it on high-quality, open-and-go curriculum. These options are more pricey, but I love that they are laid out for me and have everything I need to complete a lesson. This ensures that things get done in my house. If I have to run about gathering supplies or making copies, things are much more likely to be pushed aside. I pay for convenience.

 The best homeschool curriculum is the one that will get done.

The fact of the matter is, the best homeschool curriculum is the one that will get done. This is why it is so important to know your own strengths and limitations and work within those parameters. Initially, I bought into the idea of planning everything myself. I was convinced it would be better. After all, how else could I give my children a personalized education? The end result was that my children weren't getting a very consistent education because we were too often spinning our wheels while I tried to plan our next subject. You may be great at finding all of the most frugal deals, homeschooling with nothing but a library card, or planning out elaborate third-grade math schemes. If that's the case, then go for it. If not, know enough about yourself to find the curriculum solution that works for you.

KNOW THY CHILD

Some homeschoolers may be aghast that I put the needs of mom before the learning styles of Johnny and Suzy, but I really feel like the adage about mama being happy is true. Self-motivated second graders are the exception, not the norm, so most often, mama drives the homeschooling train, and therefore, should be considered first. Having said this, another important part of the resource equation is how your child prefers to learn.

Some kids love workbooks while others hate them. Some kids thrive on conceptual math while it reduces others to tears (I have one of each). Some kids can write for hours while others lack the fine motor skills needed to do that. Every child can learn; they just all like to do it differently. So before we press the buy button, we need to take into account how ours learn best.

Notice I said learn "best." While most people have a preferred way of learning, don't get too caught up in the idea of learning styles. In fact, the currently prevailing theory of student learning styles has not been as adequately proven as you may have been led to believe. The concept of teaching to a child's learning style is a popular buzzword in homeschool and education circles, but according to cognitive scientist and author Daniel T. Willingham, the theory has not been proven:

I've mentioned that a cognitive styles theory (learning styles) must have the following three features: it should consistently attribute to a person the same style, it should show that people with different styles think and learn differently, and it should show that people with different styles do not, on average, differ in ability. At this point, there is not a theory that has these characteristics. That doesn't mean that cognitive styles don't exist—they certainly might; but after decades of trying, psychologists have not been able to find them. (*Why Don't Students Like School?* 153)

So how do you know which curriculum will be right for your child? You know your kid. You know what he likes and doesn't like. I have come to realize that student happiness plays a role in the retention of material, while stress, on the other hand, can do a great deal to thwart learning. Whenever reasonable, I go with what makes them happy. At the same time, though, I don't feel the need to go against my own style, strengths, and limitations to cater to a perceived learning style or a child's whims and moods. I am trying to create an atmosphere, one of peace and calm, as often as possible. Happiness is more than the whims or moods of the child (or of me) at any given moment. It is a long-term state of contentment with life, with our homeschool. My goal as teacher and mom is to reach a place where we are all working together, one where my child is successfully learning and I am consistently teaching. Most often, the ability to simply do the next thing successfully gives us the greatest gains in knowledge.

MATERIALS AND RESOURCES

Beware of the gimmick trap. Tried-and-true homeschool curricula, the kind with a long track record of success and pleased customers, are tried-and-true for a reason: they're usually solid material and work for a wide variety of children. Don't be swayed by the new and shiny. The tried-and-true are tried and true for good reason—they work.

Evaluating curriculum usually means using it for a period of time. What seems great for one week sometimes becomes a dud after three or four weeks of use. Long-term evaluation of a product is important, and by all means, don't be afraid to ditch a dud and move on. Susan Wise Bauer, author of *The Well-Trained Mind*, has been known to say that if the math curriculum is making your kid cry every time you pull it out, then it is time to get a new math curriculum. There are several ways you can look through or try out a resource you are considering.

BORROW OR BUY USED

If you aren't sold on a resource but would like to give it a try, then borrowing a copy from a friend or finding a used copy is a great way to evaluate without spending a lot of money. There is a huge market for used homeschool materials, and most sellers are trustworthy and transactions go smoothly. Then, if you decide a curriculum is not for you, you can resell it as long as it is still in good condition.

Friends are a great source of information about curriculum. I have yet to meet a homeschooler who is unwilling to give a detailed opinion on the resources she has used. Almost all will be willing to let you look at and evaluate their resources, and depending on the friendship and her need at the moment, most will even let you borrow something for a few days or weeks.

BUY NEW

I know it seems contradictory, but before you buy a resource used, check out the publisher's website. Many homeschool publishers have fantastic trial periods for their resources, allowing you to buy and use curriculum for 30 or 60 days or even longer. In this case, it is much better for you to purchase directly from the publisher. That way, if the curriculum does not meet your needs, you are able to return it for a refund instead of having to deal with the hassle of reselling. Some of my favorite publishers offer such a guarantee. All About Learning has a one-year guarantee on items purchased directly from them and the Institute for Excellence in Writing has an awesome lifetime guarantee. Publishers do this because they believe in their curriculum, they care for homeschooling families, and they want you to be satisfied with your purchase. So do a little comparison shopping and evaluate the price for used versus the price for new, including the ability to return during the evaluation period.

EVALUATE AGAINST YOUR VISION AND GOALS

Perhaps the most important criteria for choosing a resource is whether or not it aligns with your vision and goals. If it is not likely to help you achieve these, then ask yourself why it's in your shopping cart. While it is easy to fill our days with the good, don't let that good squeeze out the best in your homeschool. Carefully and critically evaluate the resources you bring into your home. Strive for them to be the most useful, the best quality, and the ones most likely to move you toward your vision.

RESEARCHING RESOURCES

The number of resources available to homeschoolers these days can be absolutely overwhelming. It makes choosing which resources to use tough. Research is an important part of the process of planning.

Once you have decided which subjects you will study this year, it is time to begin researching and choosing resources. When choosing a resource to use for your homeschool, you will want to do the following:

Try to see it in person if you can. Nothing beats holding the resource in your hand and flipping through it. See all the pieces. Look at lessons in the back of the book as well as the front. You can do this by going to curriculum fairs or conventions or visiting a friend who has a copy of the resource. Some libraries also provide copies you can review.

Look at online samples. If you can't see the item in person, then be sure to spend some time looking at online samples. These will be provided on the curriculum website or many times Rainbow Resources has samples. If you do not see samples, do not hesitate to reach out to a provider via email and ask to see one. They are asking you to make an investment, so they should be willing to provide a sample.

Talk to the curriculum provider. If you have further questions, the curriculum provider is probably the best place to go for an answer. Talk to them at conventions or via their website.

Ask other moms. Moms love to dish about resources and are only too happy to tell you what worked and what didn't work. Talk to other moms in person or in online groups. Here is a list of my favorite places to get opinions about resources:

- Cathy Duffy Reviews—non-compensated!
- Favorite Facebook groups or online communities
- Here in our community
- Local friends

Be realistic. While a resource may look shiny and wonderful, you have to make sure it will mesh with your life. Here are some considerations:

Is it scripted? Do I want that script? Do I NEED that script (or other teacher helps)? There are pros and cons to both, but you can always not use the script if you don't want it. On the other hand, that doesn't work in the other direction.

How much teacher involvement is needed? For some things like phonics and most early elementary subjects, there is no getting around sitting down and teaching your kids. As they get older, they can work more independently with the right resources. Ask yourself, how much is the resource asking of you, and are you willing to make that commitment? A science experiment that is vital to understanding every lesson? Make sure you are willing to do that.

Does it require a lot of _____ that my kid doesn't like? If your kids hate cutting and pasting, skip the lap books. If they don't like to write, maybe notebooking pages aren't the thing. Got a kid who would rather read than watch a video? Skip the video-based course. While we can't cater to their needs in every area (and we shouldn't) sometimes it is better not to spend a year beating your head against the wall if other options are available.

What is the true cost? Cost is often a factor in the decisions we make about homeschool resources. As you consider the cost, realize that often, money spent is offset by the time saved. Ask yourself if spending the extra $50 will save you more than that in time spent preparing. If you have it to spend, then it might be worth the extra cost. Just be sure you factor *true*cost, which always means taking time spent into account.

The best resource is the one that gets done. Before you click the buy button, that should be the final question you ask: *Do I see this resource being used regularly (and happily) in my home this year?* If there is any doubt, at the very least you should wait on that purchase for a few days while you think it over. Consult the homeschool vision you wrote in step one to guide you as you make your decision. Make sure each and every subject you choose to study aligns with your vision. If it does not, either throw it out or adjust your vision to include it if it is that important.

ACTION ITEMS

①　Use the Course of Study form to create a Course of Study for each one of your children. If you do a number of subjects together as a family, you might want to create a separate "Family" Course of Study as well. There are two versions of the form—one that includes a column for you to include any state requirements and one that does not. Choose the one best suited to your needs.

    a.　In the subject column, label the subject your child is studying.
    b.　The schedule column is for how many days per week the child will do that particular subjects.
    c.　The notes column is for you to write your resource ideas or chosen resources.

②　Once you have decided on your subjects for the year, then you can begin to research and choose resources. Researching your options can become a time investment. You might try setting a timer and working in short chunks to keep yourself focused. You can choose a complete test or program like *Story of the World* or Apologia Science to study a subject, but don't be afraid to select a few good books and resources for some subjects. Later in this book, we will show you how to combine those and create a procedure to make your own study for any topic.

Once you have carefully considered what it is you want to study, you can begin the next steps of creating a schedule. We will cover that in the next chapter.

COURSE OF STUDY

Student: _____   Age: _____

SUBJECT	SCHEDULE	NOTES

CHAPTER 4

CREATING SCHEDULES

Homeschooling offers much freedom. There is freedom from door-to-door fundraisers, freedom from hours of homework, and perhaps most importantly, freedom in the school schedule. While most states require a set number of days for school, not a single state requires you to school on any specific day. Not having to follow the traditional school calendar gives a family an amazing amount of freedom.

For some families, like my friend Tyra's, this is the number one reason for homeschooling. Tyra's husband works odd days and shifts, and their family loves traveling to visit relatives or their favorite vacation destination: Disney. Disney during any week of summer vacation is not so much the happiest place on earth. It is hot and crowded and miserable. Disney the week after Thanksgiving, on the other hand, is a joy—ask me how I know.

 *Homeschooling offers much freedom.*

Homeschooling allows you the freedom to travel at off-peak times or simply to school on Saturday and spend time with Dad on Tuesday when he is off work. Beyond flexible vacation days, though, homeschooling allows you to create an entire schedule that works for your family. How can you be sure you are not so overwhelmed with work that learning or sanity is sacrificed? How can you best approach the material—by doing more subjects a day, or fewer? How can you create a schedule that will allow you to teach the subjects you never seem to have time to complete? Creative scheduling provides some answers. Let's take a look at a few different homeschool schedule options.

Then, let's move on to creating schedules for our year. Which days do we intend to do school? Setting our intention to do school helps us make progress even if that plan sometimes gets derailed. These frameworks we create will be structured enough to keep us on track and provide stability and motivation, but flexible enough that if we need to adjust or even pause them, we can pick up where we left off without feeling behind.

We begin plotting out our school schedules by planning from the top down and starting with our annual schedule.

TYPES OF SCHEDULES

Believe it or not, there are a number of different options for the annual school schedule. Let's take a look at a few.

TRADITIONAL SCHEDULE

This is the August through May schedule that most of us grew up with in the public school system. Based on the agrarian needs of early farmers, the method has stuck over the years. There are advantages to schooling with a traditional schedule—you take vacations when the kids in the neighborhood and the cousins do, you can participate in all of the summer activities planned for vacation months, and you probably still get a nostalgic burst of excitement and energy every fall.

One disadvantage to a long summer break is that if something happens in the middle of the school year to derail you, then you will need to extend your year into the next summer to meet the required number of school days (if you have a requirement to meet, that is).

YEAR-ROUND SCHOOLING

By tweaking the traditional schedule ever so slightly, many homeschoolers develop their own version of year-round schooling. This is what we have done at our house. We take off the end of May because that is when our swim instructor can schedule our homeschool swim lessons. We remain off during the month of June so the kids can participate in day camps and vacation Bible school. July, though, sees us getting grumpy and bored; Alabama summers are not the best for all-day outdoor play. So we usually start school right after Independence Day. We school in the morning, leaving time for indoor activities at the library or craft store in the afternoon, and then swim as it cools down in the evening.

Starting early gives us plenty of days to take off in October and March when the weather is perfect for playing outdoors. This also means we have time to take vacations when everyone else is in school. Northern friends might want to do the opposite.

CALENDAR YEAR SCHOOLING

My friend Dawn and her family school year-round, but they take off most of November and the entire month of December. Then, when the new year rolls around in January, they begin a new school year. This gives them something interesting and fresh to push them through the doldrum days of February. Note that this kind of schedule doesn't always mesh well with online classes or co-ops. You may need to adjust if you participate in those.

When you reach your halfway point of instruction in July or August, have a promotion ceremony for each student to "promote" them to their next grade level (not necessary for homeschooling, but helpful for the kids to know for church and community activities) and break out fresh, fun new school supplies from the seasonal back-to-school sales. This creative approach to the school year is only one of many possible options, and the beautiful thing is, there is no right or wrong way to do it.

SCHEDULE PATTERNS

Once you have decided when you will homeschool each year and when you will begin, then the next thing to determine is what kind of pattern you will use for your schedule. Here are some options:

TERM SCHEDULING

Both Dawn and my friend Mystie Winckler of SimplyConvivial.com use a term system. They school year-round using six-week terms, or six weeks on and one week off. Knowing she has a break coming to catch up on housework or schedule larger projects pushes Mystie through the tough times each term. She writes, "It might be tempting to skip the break week in favor of pushing on through more material, but rest and refreshment are actually important elements in the learning process." Both of these moms also have one longer period off each year as well, just not as long as the standard summer break.

Each term also contains different subjects. Mystie changes up her memory work and circle time content each term, but the variations on term work are endless. Never seem to have enough time for enrichment? Rotate art, Shakespeare, music appreciation, art appreciation, and so on each term. What about science and history? Is it hard to get to both in a week? Schedule three terms of science in a row and then three terms of history. Your schedule is only limited by your imagination.

There is nothing that says your terms must be six weeks long. You can make them longer, or they can be shorter. Your required number of school days for the year will be a factor in how short your terms can be, but there is still a large amount of flexibility there. In fact, if you make a term schedule for your year, the six-week terms will rarely line up neatly with other breaks and holidays you want to include, so your terms won't always be evenly spaced.

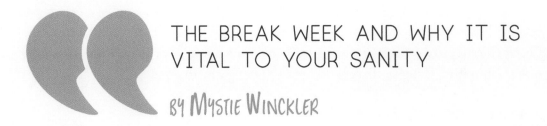

THE BREAK WEEK AND WHY IT IS VITAL TO YOUR SANITY

BY MYSTIE WINCKLER

WE HAVE OBSERVED A YEAR-ROUND SCHOOL CALENDAR from the very beginning, nine and a half years ago. We begin our school year in July, do school in six-week terms with a break between terms, taking off all of December and June. For us, the regular breaks—none of which are too long—help keep us refreshed and motivated without taking extended breaks that require lots of review time when we return to lessons.

I find a year-round homeschool calendar with regular break weeks to be a great balance, not only for the time it saves in needed review, but also because we can't keep up with the housework, we have doctor or dentist appointments, or there are other projects we'd like to do but never have time for. Such things are for break weeks.

Break weeks are profitable in their own way, too, not "wasted time." It is so easy to slip into thinking that down time or vacation time is time that doesn't "count" for anything. We say to ourselves: "I have 36 weeks of school and 16 weeks off in a year." Then we feel guilty about taking those weeks off and think maybe we should use our time better and keep getting stuff done. This mindset is not healthy.

How we and our kids spend a break week is indicative of our attitude about life, learning, and doing. We don't want to be or raise people who are only good for punching clocks and doing what they're told. If presented with time and options, what do we choose to do? That says something about us. Break weeks are diagnostic weeks, in a way: Do the kids know how to live a full life? If they only want screen time, or they whine about being bored (as several of mine did last week), it's a clue to what needs to be developed in our kids. The answer isn't giving them unrelenting checklists to keep them busy; the answer is helping them develop interests and hobbies and initiative. Lying around, being bored, wanting to be entertained by a screen isn't an indication of failure, just of what we need to be working on. Our kids are under our roof and guidance for nearly two decades for a reason: It takes a long time to help them develop good taste and habit.

Yet break week is not entirely undirected time, either. During break week we catch up on housework, cleaning bedrooms, and getting our environment back under control—a little real-world, real-life training.

During break week we often have an outing day, either spending half the day at a park or going somewhere interesting—a field trip or nature walk or play day.

During break week we work on projects. I always have more projects than I can keep up with, so I love having some time off from regular routines to do a bit of a deep dive into my current project. The kids often have project ideas of their own. Whether a lego marathon, board gaming, crafting, reading, or writing a book, they have their own ideas on how to spend their time. It's also time for reading that novel, for taking walks, for going to the park, for sleeping in. But sometimes a change is as good as a rest. Just changing things up a bit and having the time and space to delve into a necessary project feels like a break, not because it isn't work—it is!—but because it's different work, it's a different rhythm, and it feels more like "getting ahead" than the usual routine.

I have had some break week "fails"—I had one earlier this year and one or two last year. Their common issue was that I didn't get in the "preparation" stuff. If I don't deal with the piles that have collected during a term, don't do some extra cleaning (never all the extra cleaning), and a little planning and thinking about priorities for the next term, I feel like we start back up again without being ready for it, and I'm scattered and frazzled in spite of the break.

BREAK WEEK PRINCIPLE #1:
YOU WON'T GET EVERYTHING DONE

Your break week can't hold everything you want to do. If you expect to do all the fun things with the kids AND clean the house, then you're going to be sad. So we might start off break week by going to the park or doing something Monday, but spend Thursday or Friday cleaning. I find picking a theme for the days of the week helps me focus and not just flit from one thing to another.

BREAK WEEK PRINCIPLE #2:
BREAK WEEK IS FOR PREPARATION AND PLANNING

Make sure there's some significant time set aside during your break week to gather your thoughts and think through the last term, then look ahead to the next. Even if your school planning is done, you need time to review it all, pull it all together, and just wrap your head around it. When these pieces don't happen, I'm just as distracted and frazzled as I was at the end of the term.

Another thing I've noticed is that if we have a very scheduled weekend, or I'm out of town for the weekend, starting back to school on Monday is not like starting after a break. Having to jump into school mode again after being gone or in go-go-go mode is exhausting. If you have a busy out-of-the-house week during break week, then taking Monday off to gather your thoughts, make plans, and tidy up will bring more progress, sanity, and clarity in the long run than jumping straight back into the routine.

BREAK WEEK PRINCIPLE #3:
BREAK WEEK ISN'T A SABBATH SUBSTITUTE

Some call a year-round homeschool schedule a Sabbath model or Sabbath schooling. It does establish a similar ratio for our school: six weeks we labor and one we rest. However, a break week is not a rest week in the same way that Sunday should be a day of rest. Sunday is a day of worship and rest from our own agendas and plans. A break week is for a change of plans, of projects, but it's still a "make progress" week, just progress of a different kind. It's not a week of lounging and bon bons.

We do need rest, and that is why God gave us a day of rest: one in seven. Always taking Sunday as a day of rest, making that a priority, break week or not, is the most important break of all.

Breaks are flexible things. Do plan them in, but don't feel like if you aren't taking one every six weeks you're doing it "wrong." Take into account your family needs, the age spread of your family, and the weather in your part of the country, then find a flexible calendar system that provides you regular breaks from the need to direct everyone's attention and actions all day long.

FOUR-DAY WEEKS

Instead of taking week-long breaks at intervals, you can school only four days a week instead. Many homeschool families do this and take a day of the week for enrichment, housekeeping, or life. With year-round schooling, it is possible to do this and still achieve enough required days in the school year.

MAGIC NUMBER SCHEDULING

This is perhaps my favorite kind of scheduling because it provides the greatest amount of flexibility. Basically, I give myself a magic number every month—the number of days I need to homeschool that month to stay on track. I determine this number by dividing my number of required days to school each year by the number of months I am going to do school. Once I have my magic number, then I map out my months in pencil. Some months I will have more days than the magic number, and some days I know I will have less, but as long as it all averages out, I stay on track.

This way, when life happens I feel better rolling with it. I can take a couple of days off to enjoy an impromptu trip here or work on a big project there. I just aim for that magic number each month. We can't be consistent in our homeschooling unless we are hitting that average most months.

To find out if I am on track, I add up the number of days we have schooled and divide that by the number of months completed. As long as my answer is above the magic number, we are doing OK. If not, we need to work a little more the next month.

This approach takes a load off my mind and gives me the ability to flex my schedule around the unexpected and unplanned. You can also use this approach and just take a break at the end of each month—the end of the month then becomes a reward for all the hard work you have done that month.

BLOCK SCHEDULING

Similar to working in terms, block scheduling means you do fewer subjects because you are not doing every subject every term. Blocks can be of any length—six, ten, or a more conventional sixteen weeks—and means doing fewer subjects each day for a longer period of time.

Traditionally followed in high schools and middle schools, block scheduling resembles a college schedule. A student might work on composition and grammar, history, and math for one semester (about two hours a day spent on each subject) and then the following semester their subjects might include science, an elective, and literature. By the end of the year, they would still have a year's credit in each subject because they completed the number of hours needed for the credit, but by working longer hours for fewer months.

The advantage of such a system is that students juggle fewer subjects at a time. Don't underestimate the importance of this. We often work much better when we have fewer topics pulling our attention in different directions. However, the flip side is that sustained focus is required to work on a single subject for a longer period, and not all students—especially younger ones—are ready for that. Also, skills that go unused for extended periods of time are often lost, so the longer breaks between subjects—especially core areas like math and grammar—might be detrimental.

LOOP SCHEDULING

Loop scheduling is another variation that allows you to get to all of your subjects without feeling behind. Homeschool days are notoriously interrupted. Every week you manage to complete the subjects scheduled for Monday through Thursday, but for some reason, those scheduled on Friday never get done. How can we take advantage of the flexibility of homeschooling without constantly feeling behind in one or two areas? Loop scheduling to the rescue.

To create a loop schedule, list every subject you want to accomplish as part of your loop. Each day (or at the desired frequency), set aside time to work on your loop. During that time, simply pick up the loop where you last left off, work for the scheduled amount of time, and then stop for the day. You may get part of one subject done, or even two or three, and the next day you pick up the loop where you left off. Unlike scheduling specific subjects for specific days, on this plan subjects don't get skipped, and you never get behind.

The most important thing to remember when building a schedule for your school year is to do what works best for *your* family. You are not bound by requirements beyond a set number of days, so do not be afraid to be creative and come up with a plan that allows for optimal learning and family time.

WHAT IF YOU DON'T FINISH THE BOOK?

If you are meeting goals and working towards mastery, it is OK that the end of the curriculum or resource not match up with the end of the school year. While you want to be consistent and make progress, mastering a subject is far more important than checking the box, especially in skill areas. Simply close the book at the end of the year and pick up where you left off the next year.

> *Mastering a subject is far more important than checking the box.*

Action Items

① Review the six scheduling options and decide which would be best for your family. Choose what school year calendar you would like to observe:

    a. Traditional
    b. Year-Round
    c. Calendar Year

② Next, decide how you are going to break your days into segments and how you will distribute your subjects studied in each segment:

    a. Terms
    b. Blocks
    c. Loop

CHAPTER 5

PLANNING WEEKS AND DAYS

Anyone who knows me well knows I am more than a little introverted. Those who only know me a little bit really don't believe it, because I am not shy, have no problem speaking in public, and assert myself when needed. The truth of the matter is, interaction with people and being out of the home drains me, and I would prefer to just stay in most days rather than make the effort to get out into the world.

I have two children who are not at all like me, though. This means that as a homeschooling mom, I have an obligation to provide those kids with what they need: regular social interaction. This is why crafting a plan for our homeschool week takes on so many different variables and nuances. I'm not just scheduling academics, I am meeting the needs of my children. So how do I go about doing that?

> *The beauty of homeschooling is that I have the flexibility to schedule school around the other things we want to do.*

To figure out what great things will go on inside my home each week, I start with what happens outside my home. More than once, a mom has commented to me that she could never use my Weekly Plan form because she does not schedule things out so rigidly by the hour.

I laugh when I get this feedback because I don't schedule our days by the hour, either. Someone certainly could use that form to plan out which subjects they want to do at each hour every week. I'm glad it's useful in that way for those people. I use it for an entirely different purpose, though: to write in all of the times we will be out of the house during the week. For me, this is a weekly schedule of the times we will be busy elsewhere and with other things on a regular basis. By creating this schedule first, I can see the times we will be able to work on school at home.

It may seem strange to plan important academic activities around extracurriculars, but I contend that extracurriculars are important too. Since I can't teach karate myself, these activities are often determined by someone else's schedule and are not flexible. The beauty of homeschooling is that I have the flexibility to schedule school around the other things we want to do.

GETTING SPECIFIC (OR NOT) ABOUT PLANNING

Once I have established when we will be home to school each week, I can start planning what that will look like. If the last activity was about the big buckets of *when* you would be doing school during the week, this next section focuses in more on *what* you will do each day of the week. It is a slightly narrower view.

For this plan, I use the Daily Plan form to give me an overview of the week and days. Notice that the left column is labeled "Block." That is exactly how I plan my weeks/days—in *chunks* of time that have a routine duration, but not a scheduled start and end time.

I start by determining which chunks we are going to schedule. This year we have the following chunks: Morning Time, table work, and project work. These are just examples, but seeing them will help you visualize the planning process, so let me break them down for you:

Morning Time: This block is supposed to start at 9 a.m., but we are flexible with that. We all sit at the table together. and the kids draw or do something quiet with their hands while I read aloud to them. Morning Time includes narrations, grammar, foreign language, geography map work, and even handwriting instruction. Our history is also included in this time. You can read more about this efficient and relationship-building practice in my other book *Better Together: Simplify Your Homeschool, Strengthen Your Family, and Savor the Subjects that Matter Most*. My Morning Time schedule includes a combination of block and loop schedules.

Table Work: This includes those subjects where I have to provide individual instruction or the kids work independently—language arts and math for the most part. We all sit together, and I alternate working with each child while the others work independently from their own lists. When I had younger kids, sometimes I would send two of them off to play together while I finished up with another.

Project Work: This is time set aside in the day when the kids can work on their own individual interests but I am there and available to help them. We also sometimes work on art or journaling projects at this time.

Once my chunks are in place, I use the squares on the right labeled Monday through Friday to get more specific about the plans for each day. This is the point where I would caution you to avoid over-specifying what goes into some of these boxes. With a math curriculum that includes a video at the beginning of each lesson and 30 lessons scheduled for a school year, the temptation is to schedule a video every Monday, and practice sheets Tuesday through Friday. The problem with this is that it doesn't take into account my child and his ability to master the material at a faster or slower pace. By keeping things nonspecific, I will not be a slave to the curriculum or the schedule I create on this sheet. One week the child may move quickly through the material and not need practice all four days. The next he may need more than four days of practice to master the material. By simply writing math in the block,

I determine our pace, and the schedule does not. We will talk later about using lesson plan lists for subjects like math to organize how lessons are structured.

DON'T BE A CURRICULUM SLAVE
BY BRANDY VENCEL

DO YOU KNOW WHAT A CURRICULUM SLAVE IS? I'm sure you've met one before—perhaps you've been one before. (Or perhaps you're one now, in which case I'll try to help set you free in the course of this section.) A curriculum slave thinks the curriculum is her master, and she has to follow whatever the curriculum says to the letter. The curriculum slave doesn't allow herself to think about what is best for her students, or even for herself as a teacher. Instead, she exists at the curriculum's beck and call, and when she doesn't fulfill its requirements, she beats herself up.

On the other hand, we have the teacher who views herself as the master—and the curriculum is only the tool. The difference becomes obvious when we watch her in action. Yes, she uses the curriculum. After all, she "hired" it to help her do a job. But she is still the one in charge. The curriculum says Monday, but she knows Tuesday is better. The curriculum says one lesson three times per week, but she is wiser still. She knows Johnny would do best at twice that pace, while Jane would thrive on bits of lessons every day, spreading those three lessons over the course of five days.

As a homeschool mom who also writes curriculum, I think I have a unique perspective. In the beginning, I hesitated to put what I shared on my blog into a curriculum—this was supposed to be one mom sharing what she was doing with her own students. But all the emails I received from other moms convinced me that they wanted the formality and direction of a curriculum. I was happy to oblige, and yet my work is still peppered with "this is optional" and "this is not a script, but rather an example" because I want so badly for other moms to feel empowered to use curriculum as a tool, rather than exist as its slave.

But there is more to freedom than merely feeling like you have permission. The freedom a master feels comes from an intersection of knowledge and competence. The master has knowledge of the subject area, knowledge of her students, and gains experience over time.

KNOWLEDGE OF THE SUBJECT AREA

When I first started tutoring reading years and years ago, before I had children, I had a curriculum, and I followed it religiously. I don't think that was entirely a bad thing, because I was comparatively ignorant about teaching reading. At that point, the curriculum "knew" a lot more than me. It wasn't so much that I was the curriculum's slave as that I was under its instruction. The curriculum was teaching me how to teach. I needed that basic, baseline knowledge before I could get creative and improvise or change things around.

Slowly, I mastered the rules of phonics, which I had only known intuitively before. I began to understand how students learn. As my confidence in this subject area grew, so did my creativity. I added a read-aloud time, for example. The curriculum didn't call for it, but I somehow intuited that children needed to understand that books were worth reading if they were going to have a desire for literacy. I had to cut the lesson length down a bit in order to make room for that. It was the first exercise of my freedom.

Today, I have four students in four different grades in my little homeschool. It is still hard to make a call when I'm ignorant. I know, for example, that a chapter needs to be spread over three days when I've read it myself. If I haven't read it, I make all sorts of bad calls.

KNOWLEDGE OF YOUR STUDENTS

Homeschoolers and private tutors have the luxury of being able to tailor things (like pacing) to individual children and very small groups. We have the ability to know our students intimately. We know how long a lesson Johnny can handle, or exactly what number of new ideas perfectly challenges Jane without overwhelming her.

One thing you can do, if you have a student who is struggling, is keep a notebook on hand and write down your observations. The goal is to grow in your knowledge of your student so that you can make better decisions in his or her regard. I had one child, for example, who broke down at 10 a.m. on the spot every single day without exception. When I finally figured out that all she needed was a snack to help with her low blood sugar, our day was revolutionized.

Observing your students with intention will also help you know how to make time decisions on their behalf. A four-year-old likely shouldn't go over 10 minutes for his daily lessons, but a seven-year-old might do fine going over the stated 15-minute maximum to about 20 minutes. If you know your student loses all attention at minute 12, set a timer and make sure you always end right before that, regardless of whether the lesson is completed or not.

COMPETENCE

Competence comes with experience, and experience comes with time, and when we say we "learned from experience," we often mean that we learned from failure. This is where mindset comes in. You're going to make a call, and sometimes it's going to be a bad one. Accept that right now. If you spend time after that beating yourself up, you are not learning from your experience. Simply go to your mirror, look yourself in the eye, and agree that the call was a bad one and you'll try something different next time.

And then move on.

Homeschool moms are some of the most guilt-ridden, paralyzed women I've ever met, and this. needs. to. stop. (Learning to laugh at our mistakes might help.) This is not the freedom of a master. Study up, if it's your lack of subject area knowledge that is causing you to doubt yourself. Pray for wisdom and ponder your child, if it's a lack of knowledge about your student. And be confident enough to pick yourself up after you fall (and you will fall) because it's the only way to learn from your mistakes.

Be patient with the fact that you don't know it all right now. Here's a secret: no one knows it all. But you will know more in three years, and five years, and ten years, than you do now. And that's something.

So back to curriculum. It's not supposed to be a burden you carry, a slave-driver on your back telling you to hurry up and get those boxes checked. It's a tool. It's supposed to help you. So take a deep breath. Relax. Pray. And feel free to do the lessons differently from how they're written.

Because you are not a slave.

You're the master.

And the curriculum is only your hired hand.

I also find this schedule handy for writing in resources we use in addition to our main curriculum. Since we know that curriculum is what we teach and not something we buy, we might decide that one day per week we will use a different resource for math. Maybe we will use games, math readers, or a computer program. We can use this form to create a place for that in our week by writing "math books and games" under Thursday, for example.

As I continue completing each block and filling in our week, I usually determine that it is not possible to do every single subject every day—there are simply too many of them. Fortunately, we have a number of creative ways we can schedule subjects, so let's talk about traditional schedules, blocks, and loops.

TRADITIONAL SCHEDULING

This is what we remember from our school days. In traditional scheduling, you might do every subject every day, or if you think back to elementary school you might remember that you only did music once a week or history on Monday, Wednesday, and Friday. You will probably find, as you look at your subject list and resources, that most content subjects don't need to be done every single day—many homeschool science and history programs are designed to be done two or three times a week.

DAILY PLAN

Block	Monday	Tuesday	Wednesday	Thursday	Friday
Math	Math lesson Math readers	Math lesson Math games	Math lesson Math drill	Math games	Math lesson Logic puzzles
Language Arts	Spelling Composition	Grammar Composition	Spelling Composition	Grammar Composition Editing practice	Spelling Copywork
Content Subjects	History	Science	History	Science	History
Electives	Bible Study Latin Fine arts	Bible Study Latin	Bible Study Latin Fine arts	Bible Study Latin	Bible Study Art

As you can see, even some skill subjects can be done fewer than five days. For example, you can alternate spelling with handwriting—especially as kids get older and know how to form their letters. In our home, the subjects that get done every day are math, foreign language, and reading instruction.

BLOCK SCHEDULING

Block scheduling is very much like traditional scheduling except you do fewer subjects at any one time. Think back to those terms you created when you made your annual schedule. Instead of doing six or seven subjects in each term, alternate some of the subjects each term.

With blocks, you might do history in the fall terms and science in the spring terms. You are doing these subjects every day and longer each day, so you can still fit in a full year's worth of material, but you aren't tracking both subjects at the same time.

You can also use shorter terms. If you have six six-week terms in a year, maybe you do music appreciation, Shakespeare, and art for two terms each. The two terms can be back-to-back, or you can spread them out.

Here is an example of block scheduling and how content area subjects might change from term to term.

Block Schedule Planner

TERM 1	TERM 2	TERM 3	TERM 4	TERM 5	TERM 6
Math	Math	Math	Math	Math	Math
Language Arts Spelling Reading Handwriting	Language Arts Spelling Reading Handwriting	Language Arts Spelling Reading Handwriting	Language Arts Spelling Reading Handwriting	Language Arts Spelling Reading Handwriting	Language Arts Spelling Reading Handwriting
Science	Science	Science	History	History	History
Art	Art	Geography	Geography	Handicrafts	Nature Study
Spanish	Spanish	Spanish	Spanish	Spanish	Spanish

Again, I do not recommend blocking subjects like math, reading instruction, or foreign language for younger students. All subjects can be blocked in high school; many public schools do four subjects a day for a semester (typically 16 weeks) in a 1.5-hour class block. It might be beneficial to your high school student to track fewer subjects at one time.

LOOP SCHEDULING

For me, there just isn't enough flexibility in the "do this thing on this day" schedule because life is so busy. Instead, I use a loop schedule to help me get more things done and feel less stress in my homeschool.

WHAT IS A LOOP SCHEDULE?

Very simply, a loop schedule is a list of subjects you want to do in your homeschool. I always tell people when they make their loop to think about what they would like to get done in an ideal week and put about that much in their loop.

So mine might look something like this:

- Science
- History
- Shakespeare
- Art
- Geography
- Music appreciation

Notice this list is mostly content subjects. Skill subjects like math, handwriting, phonics, foreign language—the subjects that need regular or daily practice—I don't put in the loop.

Every day, when our daily subjects are done, we have a period of time in our day called Loop Time. During Loop Time I start at the top of my list and do an activity for that subject—maybe a lesson in the book or go down our procedure list for that subject. If we still have time left when we are done, we move to the next subject and do a lesson there. And so on.

When Loop Time is over for the day, we are done. We might have checked off one subject, we might have checked off three or four.

But here is the beauty: the next day, when Loop Time comes, we simply pick up where we left off and work until loop time is over again.

But if something happens—we have an emergency doctor's appointment, a chance for a cool field trip, decide to follow a fun interest or rabbit trail, or the washing machine floods—no worries. The next day we do school, we can still pick up where we left off.

It's genius! And it relieves so much stress.

The other beauty of loops is their amazing flexibility. You can use them for so many things.

Language arts is one of those catch-all subjects that really includes about five other subjects. Use a loop to include practice in grammar, vocabulary study, free writing, editing exercises, and spelling for your sixth grader.

You can also change the frequency of how often some things appear in that loop. Use the Loop Schedule Planning Form to help with this kind of frequency planning.

Let's look at the language arts loop and include some subjects more than once:

- Spelling
- Grammar
- Vocabulary study
- Spelling

- Grammar
- Free writing
- Spelling
- Editing exercises

Every day, your child is doing language arts for 30 minutes, but what they work on differs. And because of the frequency, you can see that this child is working on spelling more than, say, free writing.

Now that we have all that out in the open, I can blow your mind by telling you it is OK to combine schedule types. Some people will use blocks for some subjects, loops for others, loops within loops, and traditional scheduling as well. The possibilities are only limited by your imagination.

PLANNING OUT YOUR DAY

I wish I could tell you I have the formula for the perfect homeschool day, but sadly, I do not. All I know for sure is that there are no two homeschool days that are exactly alike, and whatever you plan, it will often not go exactly as planned.

Yet having a plan in place is important. If we don't, the overwhelming nature of the task before us will be paralyzing. So here are my best tips for creating a daily routine that inspires you to get things done. Take all of these items into consideration as you plan your blocks, loops, and chunks of time for each day.

ROUTINES, NOT SCHEDULES

Following a detailed schedule is simply not practical for most of us. Time slots on a chart are only going to frustrate us as life happens and we are constantly thrown off that schedule. So instead of a hard-and-fast block that says you will start math at 8:00 and then do reading at 8:45 and spelling at 9:10, instead, shoot for beginning your first block of work sometime between 8 and 8:30 and then have one thing follow another until you are done.

CHUNKS OF WORK

I like to call them blocks. It is easier for me to schedule in the blocks of our day instead of individual subjects. Our day typically has three big chunks—Morning Time, skill work, and project work. I do not micro-schedule within the chunks. While we complete the chunks in the same order every day, often the order within a chunk varies based on what we are doing for that subject on a given day. I always try to alternate more taxing tasks with lighter ones to give our brains a break.

MARGIN

You are never going to squeeze five hours of schoolwork into a five-hour block. Something is going to happen—the washing machine will flood, the dog will escape the fence, someone will decide this is a great day to have a stage-four math meltdown. You will not get it done, and you will end up frustrated. Schedule 3.5 hours of school work into a five-hour block. Trust me. You will thank me later.

HABIT HOOKS

Want to be sure something gets done each day? Then hang it on one of the natural hooks of your day. A natural hook is something like a meal (we all eat), naptime, a nursing session. Use these set times of things you know you will be doing as hooks for important parts of your schedule—prayer, reading aloud, memory work, art. Move right from your hook into your subject, and soon it will become a habit.

NATURAL RHYTHMS

If your family does not jump out of bed running in the morning, then resist insisting on an early start to your day. Enjoy the flexibility of homeschooling and work at your times of peak productivity. This also means taking into consideration your children's natural schedule and the fact that they have variations (which may not match yours!) as well. Got one early riser? Let him do his independent work or work with mom first. Let the others get up right before group time and then do their independent work after.

You will have an annual rhythm as well. As our mentor Damore reminds me, it's important to pay attention to your yearly rhythm—routines and lesson chunks change during busier sports season, play season, while co-op is in session, or even as the weather changes. Sometimes people get thrown off thinking that they will be able to accomplish the same lessons with the same intensity/frequency all year long and that is probably not realistic.

Homeschooling is beautiful because we don't all have to move lockstep towards the finish line— even with ourselves. Embrace it!

TIPS FOR JUGGLING MULTIPLE KIDS

Ironically the most critical barriers to your schedule are probably the people not doing school at all. When sitting to plan your routine, the infant to preschool set should be considered first in order to create a routine that will run smoothly. Some ideas:

What can you do while nursing? If baby wants to eat every morning at 8:00, then that is a great time to read aloud to the other set. Since we know reading aloud is important up until older children leave your home, gather everyone together and enjoy this time. If you can't read and nurse at the same time, then pop in an audiobook or allow an older sibling to read. In fact, nursing time is also a great time for mom to be read to, so schedule time for emerging readers to practice their skills for nursing time as well.

Trade off the toddler by making toddler care and entertainment part of the bigger kids' school time. While you work with one, the other's required task might be to play with little brother or sister and see to their needs for an allotted amount of time.

Put preschoolers first. Often a little one-on-one attention from mom goes a long way towards someone going off to happily play alone for a while. Schedule in story time and a fun activity for your twos, threes, and fours before you get started with the bigger kids.

Utilize nap time. School does not have to start early in the morning. If you have two or three young kids and one or more of them still take a long afternoon nap, then don't start school until the little ones go down. School can go from 1-3 p.m. and be done peacefully and with less frustration. Schedule the messiest, hardest, or most mom-consuming subjects for nap time.

THE BEAUTY OF BUSYWORK

Busywork often gets a bad rep in homeschool circles, but in order for our days to flow smoothly, I often have to put extra work on my kids' spiral notebook lists—this work is work they can do independently. I always make sure it is something that they need extra practice on (math facts) or is good for them to work on pedagogically (reading silently) so I don't feel too guilty that the main purpose of this independent work is to keep them engaged in school while I work with another kid.

I have found if my kids leave the table they are hard to pull back, so padding their schedule with independent activities is the best option for me. Some of these include:

- Math fact drill worksheet or app
- Other learning computer program
- Watching a lesson DVD like math or Latin
- Typing
- Reading to self or sibling
- Nature notebook
- Completing a watercolor of anything they want from their weekly readings
- Handwork projects
- Copywork
- Music practice (when the instrument is out of the room)

The more your child can legitimately do independently, the less you have to pad their lists with these optional activities. I find that if at least a third of every student's list of activities are activities they can do alone, the day balances out with me able to juggle working with all of them without losing anyone.

I always start by working with the youngest child first, trying to get him finished, and then he is able to leave and pursue his own interests. Then I work the way up the sibling ladder until only I and the oldest are left still working.

ACTION ITEMS

(1) Use the Weekly Plan form to enter in all of your outside commitments. From here, you will be able to see the hours you have available for school in your home.

(2) Next, use the Daily Plan form to determine what you will do each day of the week. Break your day into chunks—these can have descriptive names, be labeled by subject, or they can simply be labeled Block 1, Block 2, etc. Be sure to consider your family's natural rhythms and any challenges you might face.

(3) Determine which subjects you want to do in which blocks on which days, and write those into your planning form. Try experimenting with combinations of traditional, block, and loop scheduling to create a plan that works for your family.

Block Schedule Planner

TERM 1	TERM 2	TERM 3	TERM 4	TERM 5	TERM 6

Loop Schedule Planning

SUBJECT	FREQUENCY

LOOP

- _____
- _____
- _____
- _____
- _____
- _____
- _____
- _____

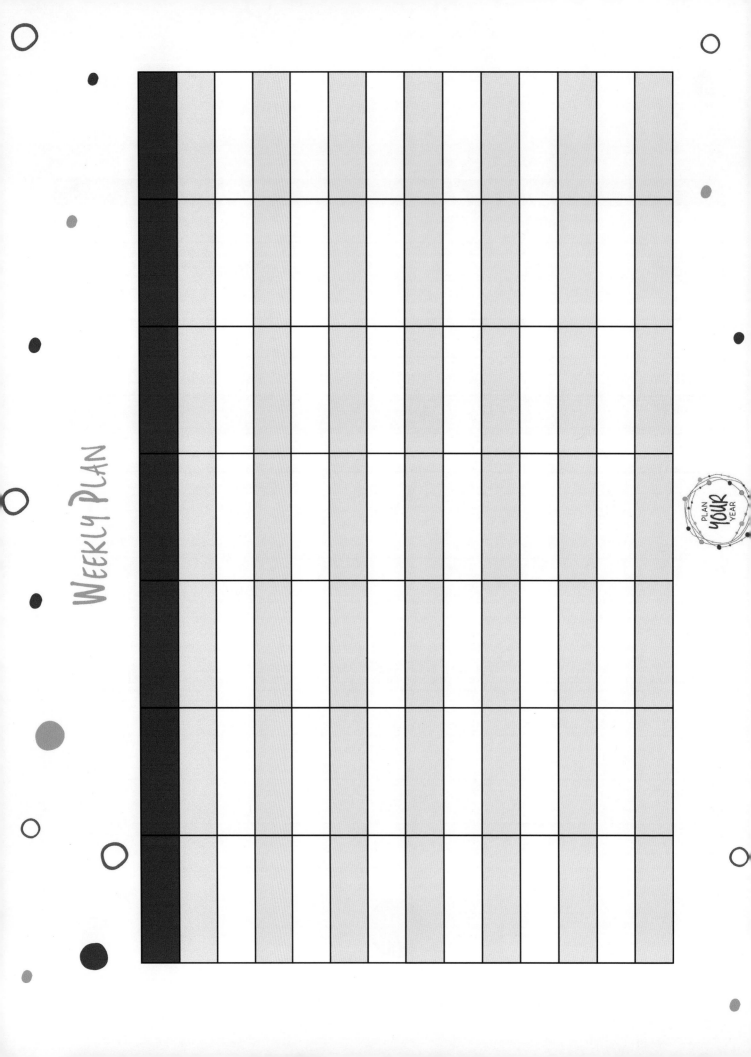

WEEKLY PLAN

PLAN YOUR YEAR

Weekly Plan

Time	Monday	Tuesday	Wednesday	Thursday	Friday
6:00					
7:00					
8:00					
9:00					
10:00					
11:00					
12:00					
1:00					
2:00					
3:00					
4:00					
5:00					
6:00					

PLAN YOUR YEAR

DAILY PLAN

Block	Monday	Tuesday	Wednesday	Thursday	Friday

CHAPTER 6

LESSON PLANNING FOR HOMESCHOOLERS

This chapter is about lesson planning, but not necessarily about writing lesson plans as you might have them pictured in your head. Instead of creating a structured grid of what we intend to do each day, we are going to create a flexible list of possibilities to guide our year. The difference is that this plan is going to flex as our life does and keep us sane. We are going to use two main kinds of lists in this chapter for our lesson plans.

Most of us can remember our teachers and their green-shaded, double-page lesson planner book, right? The one that was always open in the middle of their desk or podium? Since I'm a homeschool teacher, I need a fancy lesson plan book just like that. Something that tells me exactly what we are going to be doing every day of the week. Or do I?

Before you get mired down in the idea of a complicated homeschool planner, consider the purpose of teacher lesson plans. As a public school teacher, I made plans to turn in to my department head. Sure I worked from the plans, but putting them into separate boxes, labeling them with which objectives they tried to meet, and organizing weeks at a time wasn't something I did because it was practical, but because it was required by the system. I turned in lesson plans so the system could hold me accountable and cover its bottom. I can't tell you how many times something caused me to deviate from those plans, and I had to redo them. Does this sound familiar?

The good news is that even those of us working under more stringent state requirements don't need to create complicated daily lesson plans for our homeschools. Instead, something far simpler and more helpful will work.

In the past few years "list-checking" has gotten a bad reputation in the homeschool community, but despite that fact, the best lesson planner for homeschooling is really the humble list. Here is how you can use three kinds of lists for your homeschool, to keep you on track every day.

THE PROCEDURE LIST

I love using open-and-go curriculum as much as possible. My favorite programs are the ones that tell me exactly what to do next so I don't even have to think about it. You may choose to use a few of these kinds of programs in your homeschool to make your life easier. But sometimes I want to use a resource that is is fabulous albeit not so friendly to the decision-fatigued mom. For those programs, I need a procedure list.

A procedure list is a simple tool that tells me exactly what to do in order to teach from any subject or resource. I make these magical lists myself, so they only include the things I want my kids to practice, do, or study. They eliminate the need for me to think or wonder what is next when we study a particular subject. All the information I need is included on the list.

WHY CREATE A PROCEDURE LIST?

Let's look at a few situations where a procedure list might come in handy.

The curriculum has an overabundance of choices.

Maybe it has too many moving parts to choose from, like the *Story of the World Activity Book*? There are so many choices in that book that if I waited until I started to study each chapter and then tried to choose our activities, I would never begin history. I know my family will never do all the things in that book, so I am better served by determining what we will do up front and leaving the rest out.

The book has no guide at all.

The Burgess Bird Book for Children is an example. This book is a wonderful introduction to birds, but I always feel like I need to add something to it to make it a fuller study. If I add a few resources like the Dover Birdwatcher's Coloring Book, a bird sounds app or device, and maybe some bird notebooking pages, I can create a study using simple procedures that will add to the book in a meaningful way. You can use this method to create your own mini-curriculum from any collection of resources.

It is a practice that doesn't require a curriculum.

This would be something like reading poetry, writing narrations, or practicing map tracing. A curriculum for these things might be overkill, but a procedure list helps you visualize and create a series of steps to practice these skills regularly without having to create the lesson from scratch each time.

EXAMPLE OF A PROCEDURE LIST

So back to *Story of the World*. Here is an example we used for that a few years ago:

1. Write names and place names from the chapter on a whiteboard.

2. Listen to the chapter while completing a coloring page.

3. Provide oral narration of part of the chapter. Use questions and names on the whiteboard as needed.

4. Look up the topic in *The Usborne Encyclopedia of World History*. View any interesting Internet links.

5. Complete map work.

That wonderful activity book I talked about is full of so much information and so many things to make and do, I get a little overwhelmed by it all. So I made my own list of what I want to do each time we study a *Story of the World* chapter. It took just a few minutes to come up with the plan, decide on the resources to use, type up the list, and print it. That list then goes into my binder, and I refer to it until the procedure becomes second nature.

The beauty of creating my own simplified procedures for these subjects is that in the heat of the moment, I don't have to think about what I want to do to study a specific subject—it is all laid out for me on the page. This makes all the difference in the world for consistency and follow-through on a subject. With all the distractions that surface in my day, I know exactly what to do next, even if my brain is hurting. I create procedures for every subject that doesn't come with step-by-step instructions and for which I feel the best way to present the material is to follow the same steps over and over.

Here are a few ideas for procedure lists to get you started.

- Map drawing or tracing
- Music appreciation
- Picture study
- State or country study
- Animal, plant, or bird study
- Freewriting

Making procedure lists is easy. Here is exactly how you do it:

1. Gather your all your resources for a specific subject. Books, texts, notebooking pages, lapbooks—whatever you have.

2. Think carefully about your goals for that subject. It might be helpful to grab a goals worksheet and jot down a few goals. For a geography study, my goals might be for the kids to be able to name each state and capital, place the states on a map, and remember at least one interesting tidbit about each state.

3. List out the procedure you want to follow. Be sure to list the steps in the exact order you want to do them. Consider your goals, and don't add extra things despite the temptation to pile on more—only list what you will honestly do and what will meet your goals.

4. Finalize your list and keep a copy handy. You can type these and print them to put in a teacher binder, put them on a clipboard with your attendance sheet, or write them on index cards and store them on a ring. Do whatever you need to do to keep them close by so you will use them.

The possibilities for using procedures are endless, and the end result is a more peaceful mom.

I can't keep the chaos from happening, but I am better prepared to deal with it. All I have to do is open my binder and do the next thing.

THE LESSON PLAN LIST

Sometimes a procedure list doesn't work perfectly for a subject. In cases where you want to add more variety to lessons, you might need a detailed lesson plan list. Let's look at an example of one of these.

Let's say you are studying the Middle Ages this year with your upper elementary kids and want a resource that makes things easy for you but still allows you to meet your goals. So you get *Famous Men of the Middle Ages* from Memoria Press along with the teacher's guide (easy for you).

A procedure list for that book and workbook might look like this:

1. Read or listen to the chapter.

2. Define the vocabulary (orally) in your own words.

3. Answer the comprehension questions in complete sentences.

4. Do the map work and timeline work.

5. Choose one of the additional activities to complete, if available.

But what if you don't want to study all 34 of the people, you want to add more women to the mix (Eleanor of Aquitaine, anyone?), or you don't think all of the exercises in the student book have equal value?

You might sit down at your word processor or spreadsheet program and come up with a list that looks like this:

Lesson 1: Attila the Hun

1. Read pp. 19-21 in the book. Do oral narration.

2. Add Orleans, Chalons, Aquileia, Venice, and the Adriatic Sea to map. Color.

3. Add Attila to Middle Ages timeline.

4. Watch YouTube video.

Lesson 2: Theodoric the Ostrogoth

1. Read pp. 29-31 in the book. Do written narration describing the two sieges of Ravenna and the murder of Odoacer.

2. Add Ravenna, Aquileia, Verona, the Black Sea, and the Adda River to map.

3. Update timeline.

4. Create a comic strip or notebooking page that illustrates and describes the siege of an ancient city. Research using YouTube or books.

Lesson 3: Benedict and Gregory

1. Read pp. 33-35 in the book. Narrate either Benedict's or Gregory's life.

2. Add Monte Cassino to the map.

3. Make your own "rule" for your daily life. What are some practices you would follow?

4. Listen to a Gregorian chant on YouTube.

And so on. I made this list largely using the activities in the *FMMA* teacher's guide, leaving out many activities and adding a few of my own. I continued until I had created a lesson plan list for the entire book. This kind of lesson plan list is extremely flexible. You can create one to accompany textbooks, or you can compile a few random resources around a topic and use those resources to create a list (see Chapter 7 for more on how to do this).

It is a good deal of work up front, but keep in mind this is what will reduce decision fatigue and free up time during your school year—making all the decisions up front and then having them ready to follow through the year.

A few important notes on making your lists:

1. As with procedure lists, make sure you keep your vision and goals in mind and resist the urge to pile on. Remember that a few well-chosen, quality activities are better than trying to do all. the. things. Leave margin in your plans—for rabbit trails, your kids' interests, and even life.

2. Notice there are no dates anywhere here. We will get on to assigning these lessons in a later chapter, but for now, they are just ordered, undated, lists.

3. Save these lists! You might use them again in other years and with other kids.

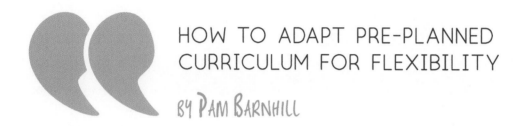

HOW TO ADAPT PRE-PLANNED CURRICULUM FOR FLEXIBILITY

BY PAM BARNHILL

I am all about convenience, and nothing is more convenient than a resource that plans out multiple subjects for you and integrates them together. They can make life very easy. But as we saw in Brandy Vencel's article in the previous chapter, the goal is not to become a slave to the resource you have chosen, but instead to master it, using it in the way you see fit. So how do you do this when these resources are laid out in grids without making a complete and total mess of your pre-made lesson plans, ending up with multiple bookmarks, cross-outs, and the nagging question, "Where are we now?" as you glance at the lesson grids. Below are three solutions that will help you master the prepared curriculum.

SOLUTION 1: STRIP THE CONTENT OFF THE GRIDS

This is the most time-intensive solution, but some personality types will be willing to put in the extra work in exchange for the neatness of the final product. Use a spreadsheet or word processing program and simply retype the lessons for each subject onto a new page, essentially creating a detailed lesson plan list from the content. Use each subject's list in your day as you would a lesson plan list you created yourself.

SOLUTION 2: WORK ACROSS AND EMBRACE THE BOOKMARKS

If you view the pre-made lesson plans by subject, looking across the grid instead of by day (looking down) then you really already have the lesson plan list made. So cover up the day designation at the top of the columns, and view your next thing to do by looking across the subject rows. When it is time to do that subject in your schedule, do the next thing. This will allow you to easily combine your pre-made resource with traditional, block, and loop scheduling of your own choosing instead of having to do what the curriculum provider desires. Inevitably, with this method, you will end up on multiple pages of the resource. You can use colored paper clips or colored sticky tabs (assign each subject its own color) to help you quickly find your place.

SOLUTION 3: MAKE A GIANT LOOP SCHEDULE

Use the lesson grid as a giant, snaking, loop schedule. Start at the top with Day 1 and the first subject and work your way down the first column. Go as far as you can, doing each subject in turn, until school is done for the day. The next day, when you start school again, pick up where you left off. Some days you may get in more than a day's "worth of work" and others you may get in less, but with consistency, those days will even out, and you will move through the curriculum without getting behind or neglecting any particular subjects.

THE SIMPLE LESSON PLAN LIST

Earlier in the chapter, we taught you how to make procedure lists for all of your curriculum that isn't open-and-go. If you do that, you now know exactly what you will do when you sit down to do a lesson. In addition to those procedure lists, you can make a simple lesson plan list and use it to mark off what you have completed as you work through your curriculum. This lesson plan can be as easy as making a photocopy of the table of contents of your curriculum and storing it with your procedure list. Let me give you an example of how this would work.

You have decided that you want to study Song School Latin 2 with your fourth grader and second grader this year. SSL has a ton of wonderful resources available—so many that it makes your head spin a bit—so you create a procedure list that looks something like the "Song School Latin Lesson Procedure List" on page 86:

Song School Latin Lesson Procedure List

Day One:

1. Watch the DVD of the lesson.

2. Sing the lesson song and review one other song from a previous chapter.

Day Two:

1. Review vocabulary (use pronunciation audio files if needed), song (new and one other review), and discuss Famous Saying, Chapter Lesson, and Grow Your English sections.

2. Complete Practice Your Latin and one workbook page.

Day Three:

1. Listen to song (new and one other review)

2. Play Latin Monkey Match with new cards and a selection of cards for review.

Day Four:

1. Listen to song (new and one other review)

2. Complete the final workbook page.

Day Five:

1. Listen to song (new and one other review)

2. Play Headventureland

This is exactly how you are going to do Latin for every lesson, so to stay on track with what you need to do next, you really just need a photocopy of the table of contents in the teacher's guide so you can mark off each lesson as you complete it. Easy-peasy.

THE EASIEST "LESSON PLAN"

For an open-and-go curriculum—one that is scripted like All About Reading or "do the next thing" like Math-U-See—I don't even do the work of photocopying the table of contents and making checkmarks. Instead, I use a bookmark that shows me where to begin each day. We either set a timer or work to their tolerance level, and then I put the bookmark back in to indicate where to begin the next day.

If you live in a state that requires written plans showing what you did each day, you can simply keep a more formal lesson planning form handy and write in exactly what you did after you complete it each day.

ACTION ITEMS

1. Use the Lesson Plan Requirement List form to divide your curriculum into three categories. 1) Open-and-go. 2) Procedure and simple lesson plan list. 3) Detailed lesson plan list. Congratulations! You are now finished with the open-and-go column!

2. Take a good look at your subjects and resources, and decide which ones would benefit from a procedure list. Keeping your goals for each subject in mind, follow the steps outlined earlier in the chapter and create a procedure list for each of these subjects.

3. Next, create detailed lesson plan lists for each subject in the third column. These will be the most time-consuming, but in turn, will save you the most time during the school year.

4. If you are using a prepared curriculum, determine how you will organize the materials to best meet your needs.

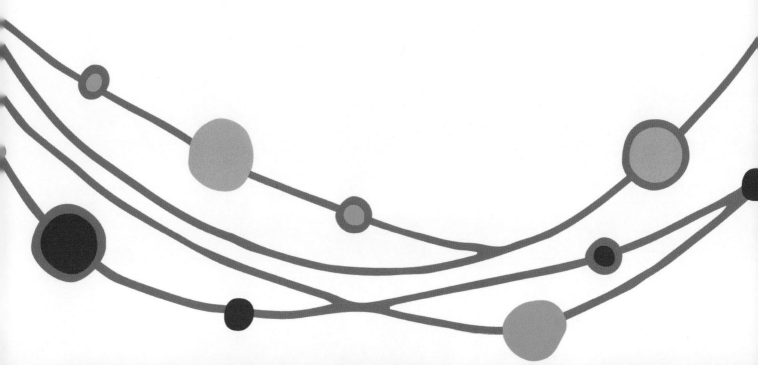

Lesson Plan Requirement List

OPEN-AND-GO	PROCEDURE LISTS	LESSON PLAN LISTS

Procedures

Subject: _____

- _____
- _____
- _____
- _____
- _____
- _____
- _____
- _____
- _____
- _____
- _____
- _____
- _____
- _____

Lesson Plan List

Subject: _____

LESSON	RESOURCES	ACTIVITIES

CHAPTER 7

PLANNING YOUR OWN STUDY

As a young homeschool mom, I had the misconception that if I was not planning every subject from scratch, I was somehow short-changing my kids. This could not have been farther from the truth. In fact, my kids' educations were suffering because, in a frenzy, I would get a few weeks of math or reading planned out, we would complete the work, and then we would spin our wheels not doing much until my next burst of energy came along and I could finish planning the next bit. It didn't take me long to embrace the pre-planned resources I now use and love.

Having said this, sometimes I can't find a lesson plan that I think we will enjoy, or I find one I know I will have to tweak until it looks like a shell of its former self. Sometimes I find a book or resource that looks too good to pass up, but there are no lesson plans to go with it. Or I find an entire collection of resources on a topic that all look great, but I end up wondering how I can fit them together to make my own mini-curriculum. There are so many wonderful books, videos, games, lapbooks, and activities available. When this happens, I create my own study using procedure lists and lesson plan lists. When you use those two tools, it isn't hard to do at all. In this section, I'm going to show you how.

PICK A TOPIC

First you have to choose a topic. This is where your overall goals and requirements come in handy. Is your topic Oregon state history because you have a state requirement to study that? Great. But what if you just want to introduce your elementary age students to the study of history? It is perfectly OK in this sense to choose a topic like "Egyptians," "Explorers," or "Cowboys." You do NOT have to start off with a huge era like "Ancient History." There is no reason why an early elementary child needs to study large sweeps of history in a year when they would likely engage more with deeper dives into smaller topics and time periods with many opportunities to study the people and events of that time period. For content area subjects (see Chapter 3) in the younger grades, simply choose topics they will enjoy.

Even in the older grades, you can choose to study a subject like biology or American History via a collection of resources or books instead of using a curriculum.

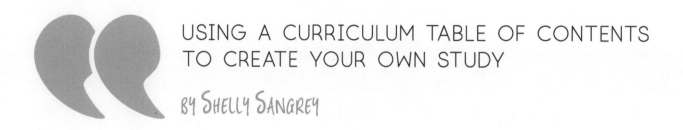

USING A CURRICULUM TABLE OF CONTENTS TO CREATE YOUR OWN STUDY

By Shelly Sangrey

I have a love/hate relationship with textbooks. On one hand, they're dreadfully dull and lifeless. On the other, they often contain lots of great information; the problem is how it's presented.

I think most people have a very narrow view of how a textbook should be used: Read it, complete the review questions and vocabulary, take a test.

Ugh. Can you say b-o-r-i-n-g?

Thankfully, textbooks don't have to be used a certain way. As inflexible as they may seem, it is entirely possible to tailor them to suit your family's needs.

Here's one way to do that.

HOW TO USE A TEXTBOOK FLEXIBLY

When most people think of a textbook, they think of the body of text. When I think of a textbook, I think of the table of contents.

Sound strange?

Think about it. The table of contents gives an overview of what material will be covered in a given resource. Each and every major topic that will be touched upon is listed out, often with subheadings giving even more detail.

But what if you looked beyond that? What if, instead, you used that one item as the spine for a custom-made curriculum that is designed for your child and not a multitude of children?

Here are some ideas of how this can be accomplished. (The first suggestion is the only one I feel is absolutely necessary. The rest are simply ideas you might consider.)

Make a list of all of the topics listed in the table of contents.

For example, I have a biology book in which the following areas are covered in the first chapter:

- Flowering seed plants
- Structure and function of leaves
- Flowers, fruits, and seeds
- Stems and roots
- Plant varieties

The list you come up with will comprise the framework for the following activities.

Head to the library and gather some books (not textbooks) that cover the items on your list.

Have you ever noticed how much more interesting actual books are than textbooks? You can easily cover the same information contained in a textbook by using the library instead. Just because something's interesting doesn't mean that it's any less educational. In fact, I think the exact opposite is true.

Compile a notebook to write about the books the kids read.

There's just something about a child getting to choose what they're going to write about a subject than being asked review questions at the end of a chapter. It brings with it a sense of ownership. This can be a fabulous outlet for kids who don't like to write because there are so many options to include in a notebook, such as:

- Pamphlets
- Maps
- Drawings
- Comic strips

- Creative writing (focusing on the subject at hand)
- Glossaries
- Reviews
- Anything else you think of

Incorporate hands-on activities to solidify what they've learned.

Thanks to Pinterest, you can find hands-on activities for just about anything. Be creative! If your child is learning about seeds, plant a garden. If they're learning about weather, make a tornado in a bottle. If they're studying pioneer times, make a recipe from that era. There are millions of ideas out there!

Plan field trips connected to the topics you're studying.

Field trips are another great way to help a child make connections with what they're learning. And keep in mind that they needn't be expensive. Consider heading out into the woods to look for animal tracks, visiting a nursery or a local farm, or wading in a creek to hunt for clutches of frog eggs. I guarantee this will beat simply reading about the subject in a textbook any day.

Find some good movies or videos to supplement the material.

I'm not one for using the TV every day during homeschool, but I do believe there is a huge variety of visual media that can be extremely beneficial when combined with other learning approaches. Consider the subject you're teaching/learning and search Netflix, YouTube, Amazon Prime, or your public library for documentaries or other relevant programs that may interest your child.

Combine all of the above!

I think this one's self-explanatory.

As tedious as I think textbooks are, there's no doubt that they can be a great guide or jumping off point on which to base your very own tailored curriculum. Simply stick with the table of contents, frame your lessons around it, and you can be well on your way to your very own customized homeschool. Now that's an approach to textbooks I can handle.

CREATE GOALS SPECIFICALLY FOR *YOUR* STUDY

Before you begin creating your own study—let's say, one on Shakespeare—start by jotting down a few goals. What is it, exactly, that you want your kids to learn about this topic? Why is it important for you to study it? Knowing what you are trying to accomplish will guide you in choosing the books and creating the activities. For my Shakespeare study, I listed my goals and a few of their related activities and books below.

- **Students will understand that Shakespeare is important because of his vast contributions of words, idioms, and allusions to English language and culture.**

  - Read *Will's Words* picture book on how Shakespeare's writing has impacted the English language.
  - Watch *Horrible Histories* skit illustrating the phrases Shakespeare added to everyday life.

- **Students will become familiar with Elizabethan theater and culture.**

  - Participate in The Globe escape room activity and search London for a missing play script.

- **Students will experience watching and reading a play by Shakespeare and use it to practice literary analysis.**

  - Listen to the Archangel version of *The Tempest* and discuss.

- **Students will have fun with Shakespeare.**

  - Weekly game show-style quiz about the events of each act of the play.
  - Participate in Shakespearean insult slam.

These are not all of my activities for the study, but they do give you an idea of how I have chosen what to do based on the goals I want to accomplish.

Use the goal writing process in Chapter 2 to help you create your goals, but don't overthink them. Remember my geography study goals from the last chapter? They were simply for the kids to be able to name each state and capital, place the states on a map, and remember at least one interesting tidbit about each state. It can be as simple as that.

FIND A FEW GOOD BOOKS

Spend a little time in homeschooling circles, and it won't be long before you come across the term "living book." Coined by 19th-century educator Charlotte Mason, a living book is written by a single author, provides information in a narrative style, and uses rich language. It doesn't talk down to children or dumb down information. It is not dull. It is a book that will capture your attention with its quality, even if you have little interest in the topic at first.

This is the kind of book we want to use with our children. While it is sometimes tempting to reach for the first book the library has on hand, this often defeats the purpose of engaging our children. When I look for a book, I look for one that uses rich language, imagery, and interesting vocabulary, even in a nonfiction work. I search for beautiful artwork in a picture book as opposed to cartoonish drawings. We love picture books that are illustrated in an artistic manner using techniques like collages, woodcuts, or watercolors.

Here is an example from a book about the monarch butterfly. The book, *Hurry and the Monarch*, tells the story of an unlikely friendship between a turtle and a monarch butterfly. Woven into the narrative, we learn about the monarch's migratory pattern, its dependence on the milkweed plant, and its life cycle from caterpillar to butterfly, which is illustrated beautifully with detailed watercolor paintings. From the book:

> But the monarch survives, flying now toward Eagle Pass, over the waters of the Rio Grande into Mexico. On and on she flies until finally, one November evening, she finds it. The warm green forest she has been searching for. She hangs from a bough, adding her tired wings to the soft murmur of a million others.

Compare this to *Butterfly and Moth* by Paul Whalley:

> The Monarch travels from Canada and the Eastern seaboard across America to its winter quarters in California and Mexico. Having survived the winter, the butterflies then fly back north.

Which book is more likely to engage your imagination and curiosity?

If you have young kids, you are in for a treat with all the books available on the topics you will study. There are books on rocks, animals, kings, presidents, places—any topic you can think of. Name a topic you want to study, and there is likely a great book on it. In fact, I would encourage you to skip the complicated science and history curriculum in the youngest grades and just focus on reading interesting books. At this point, you may be wondering how you are going to find them all. In truth, it is really all about accessing resources. There are many, many book collections available online, and a quick Google search will help you find them.

An important thing to remember is that most booklists are simply too long. Do not attempt to read every book on any list, but instead choose the best books to savor and enjoy. We tend to think that if one book on the Civil War is good, then five must be even better, but that is usually not the case. Choose carefully and allow your children to ruminate over one well-written book instead of flooding them with a multitude of mediocre choices.

DIFFERENT BOOKS FOR DIFFERENT PURPOSES

By Pam Barnhill

Creating a booklist begins by determining the purpose of the list. Are these books you will read aloud to your children, books your child will read independently, or books you'll use to study a particular content area like history or science? Differing purposes have a large impact on the kinds and number of books we will choose.

READ-ALOUDS

Never underestimate the importance of reading aloud to your children right up until the time they leave your home. One of the biggest mistakes we make as parents is that we stop reading to our children once they are able to read independently. Reading aloud to older children exposes them to vocabulary and language patterns beyond their own reading ability. It demonstrates the family's value of reading and books and is an enjoyable family pastime. For more benefits on the importance of reading aloud to kids of all ages, I encourage you to spend about an hour listening to the Read-Aloud Revival Podcast, Episode 1, wherein writing teacher and homeschool speaker Andrew Pudewa explains the importance of continued reading aloud.

Read-aloud books should be chosen for enjoyment, exposure to classic literature and rich language, and enjoyment (that was worth repeating). You can find great books for reading aloud from the lists in Sarah Mackenzie's *The Read Aloud Family,* a fabulous resource to have on hand for your homeschool. Simply choose something from the list that looks interesting to get you started, or maybe a favorite from your own childhood. Then set a goal to read aloud for a certain number of minutes each day. Once you finish one book, simply move to another on the list.

I typically try to read aloud books that are above my kids' own reading levels—books they could not read to themselves. Kids are able to understand and enjoy classic novels with rich language and complex plots if we work at it a bit. I sometimes find that playing more difficult books to a captive audience and with a professional narrator (read: audiobooks in the car) helps them get used to more challenging selections.

INDEPENDENT READING

If I seem a bit like a reading snob, it's possible you may think me the opposite after this section. When kids are learning to read fluently, they need to read and read and read and read some more. At this point, I loosen my expectations that they will read quality books quite a bit. While I don't completely abandon my standards, I do allow binges on things like fairy books and comics as long as much reading is being done.

I also encourage children's adaptations of classic works for young readers. My eight-year-old daughter sat on the edge of her seat for an entire three-hour production of Shakespeare's *A Midsummer Night's Dream* because she was familiar with more than one children's adaptation. Bring on the abridged version first, I say.

Mostly, though, selecting books for young readers means selecting a few quality novels written at their reading level, which may or may not be the same as their grade level. You can have kids use a five-finger test to see if books are right for them. To do this, have a child turn to a page in the middle of the book and read it. They can put one finger up for every word they can't read or don't understand. More than five fingers up at the end of the page? Choose another book and use this one as a read-aloud. Fewer than five fingers? The book should be just right.

Readers should be encouraged to read heavily below their own reading level to build fluency and satisfaction. Books for "school" and discussion should be at their reading level, while books above their reading level should be used as read-alouds. Many libraries provide a reading level assessment on the spines of their juvenile fiction books to help you determine reading level. There are age recommendations on bookselling websites like Amazon. The Scholastic Book Wizard also allows you to search by reading level.

Independent reading falls into two categories: books a child reads for enjoyment or exposure and books a child reads for discussion. You, as the parent, may want to make a list of books you would like your child to read independently this year. Choose three or four to begin with. Hopefully your child will read that list and more. Encourage this with frequent trips to the library and bookstore.

When you're assigning books for independent reading, be sure to take into account all the reading your kids are required to do across the curriculum so as not to overload their schedules. It bears repeating that engagement with and contemplation of a few great books is more desirable than rushing through a large list to simply mark them off and say they were read.

LITERATURE STUDY

These are the books you will use with older kids (middle school and up) for instruction in figurative language, plot, and character analysis. Before the middle school years, just make it your goal to simply enjoy books with your children. There is no need to pick apart everything they read at a young age—let them learn to love books instead.

I encourage you to limit the number of books you choose for literary discussion to those you can read yourself. It is impossible to discuss or teach a book you have not read. If I ambitiously assign five books to each of my three children, then I need to be prepared to read fifteen books on my own this year. That's quite a few books for a busy mom to read. Instead, encourage a large amount of independent reading and limit the assigned reading to two or three quality choices per child.

My favorite resource for discussing literature with my children is Teaching the Classics by Adam and Missy Andrews. The Andrewses lead you through how to choose good books, they teach you literary analysis (helpful if it has been a few years since your last college literature class), and they provide a list of questions to ask your children about the books you read.

FINDING RESOURCES ON YOUR TOPIC

Once you have a content area topic to study, begin by creating a list of subtopics. The Middle Ages might include subtopics like knights, King Arthur, castles, cathedrals, the crusades, religious life, and so on. Space would include books on the sun, the planets, stars, the moon, and space travel. Search the booklists for age-appropriate books on each subject. There is no reason to reinvent the wheel when there are so many good resources available. You may discover there is one website or booklist you come to appreciate more than others. Use that one as your go-to aid in choosing books. Amazon and homeschooling blogs (search for the book title and the word "review" via Google) are a great source for book reviews. And be sure to peruse the shelves of your local library to preview selections.

In most cases, you will end up with a large selection of books from which to choose. Then you will need to whittle down the list to fit within your time constraints. Count the total number of chapters/ picture books you intend to read, and divide it by the number of weeks you will be doing school. Then evaluate whether or not this is a reasonable amount of reading to do each week. If not, cull the list by foregoing some books or moving others to the independent reading list if there is room there. If you are having a hard time getting your content area list whittled down, never underestimate the value of strategically placing a few of the books where your kids will find them. You may find that they pick up a few and read them on their own. I call this technique "stealth schooling." It is also known as "strewing" in unschooling circles.

Once you have books for your subtopics, you can add in a few additional resources. While a great study can be designed only around books, you might find these other resources enjoyable as well:

- Documentaries
- Games
- Apps
- Puzzles
- Lapbooks
- Notebooking pages

- Activities from Teachers Pay Teachers
- Experiments, kits, and crafts
- Primary source documents
- Online classes
- Field trips and local classes

Whichever of these you decide to use will depend largely on your philosophy of education and what you and your kids enjoy doing. Remember, there is no right or wrong answer. Do what makes learning fun and effective for *your* family.

MOVING FROM RESOURCES TO PLAN

Once you have this large pile of books and fun resources in front of you, it is time to make them into a useable plan for your study. You do this by either creating procedure lists or lesson plan lists (see Chapter 6). Either method of lesson planning will work well, the lesson plan list will just give you more variety. As an example, let's say that you want to study animals with your second grader. So you choose a few resources to use:

- *The Usborne World of Animals* (internet linked)
- Animal Notebooking Pages from notebookingpages.com

- *The Story of Dr. Dolittle*
- Map of the world

Creating a study would be as simple as making a procedure list which might look something like this:

1. Alternate days: read 4-8 pages from *The Usborne World of Animals* OR 4-8 pages of *The Story of Dr. Dolittle.*

2. Narrate by telling back.

3. Find any named locations on the world map.

4. As you come across interesting animals in your studies, choose some to include in your book of animals. Daily during the study, create a page for each animal by drawing a picture and writing (or copying) two to three facts about the animal on the page.

If you follow this procedure list, it will take about 60 school days to complete your study. You can build in margin by allowing yourself to work on this over the course of an entire semester. This will allow you to slow down and pull in extra resources if a child becomes interested in a topic or animal. It will also allow you to not stress on the days that second grader melts down and won't write his animal facts.

Alternately, let's say you also find a wonderful packet of Animals Around the World games, activities, and notebooking pages online. Instead of the procedure list, you can create a lesson plan list by using a spreadsheet program. Begin by listing your readings down the first column (divide them just as we did in the procedure list example) and then in the next column, list the activities you will do from the activity packet. Which days will you play games, which will you do notebooking pages, which will you do map work? Which activities go best with what you read that day?

Let me stress that even though you will be mapping out what you are doing each day, don't add dates to this list—just numbers to keep things in order. You may still end up with 60-70 days of activities on your list and can work your way down, doing them over the course of a semester and still allowing for margin. Planning things out like this is a little more work up front, but your completion rate grows exponentially with this advance planning.

YOU DO YOU

Planning out your own studies is not for everyone, nor is it necessary for successful homeschooling. Some homeschoolers will absolutely love this step while others would rather have their fingernails removed. It's OK either way. There are plenty of great free and paid curriculum options out there that do this work for you already. Choose one of those, open it and use it as is, or tweak it to fit your family. I do a mix of both, because I enjoy the planning process immensely but also understand the limitations on my time. When I find something I like, I use or adapt it. When I don't, I make some plans. But I don't lose any sleep over any of it.

ACTION ITEMS

① Make the decision—is there a curriculum available that you would be happy using or tweaking, or do you want to design your own study for this subject?

② Once you have decided to design a study, gather your books and other resources.

③ Decide if you will use a procedure list or lesson plan list for your study.

④ Write out your plans.

CHAPTER 8

ORGANIZE YOUR MATERIALS

When we moved into our last home years ago, I was certain the upstairs bonus room would be the perfect place to homeschool. The room was large and open with ample space for shelves and a table. However, I quickly discovered that the carpeted floor meant it wasn't right for messy activities. Plus, we were cut off from the rest of the house where the baby was napping or the snacks were kept or the laundry needed moving.

Gradually, our homeschool migrated down to our breakfast nook in the kitchen. I set up a few small shelves under the bar counter, and we schooled in that room, did art in that room, and ate in that little bitty room. Just one open door away, the formal dining area sat unused. Visible from the front door, the dining area was a place I tried to keep neat and tidy with its formal black table and lighted china cabinet full of creamy white dishes. Often the unused table became a dumping ground for mail and books because no one ever sat there or used it. Then I got over myself.

I stopped trying to live the picture in my head of the perfect home and started living the reality that was our life. I moved my shelves and my students into that formal dining area and stopped worrying about what people might think when they came through our front door for the first time. We homeschool, and it permeates our entire family culture. For a year, we lived there with our little shelves, traveling back and forth up the stairs for the rest of our supplies. We did everything on that dining table with the fabric-covered chairs and the china as our backdrop. I cringe when I think about it now, but I was making do with what I had. We had found our perfect space.

Finally, we sold the formal dining room furniture on Craigslist and made the pilgrimage so many homeschoolers make: to IKEA. We used the funds from our resold furniture to outfit the room to meet our needs. We couldn't be happier with the result. That's the main thing right there: *we are happy*. It doesn't matter what kind of schoolroom you have or don't have; the important thing is to work at making it a space where you can be happy and function. My friend Mystie Winckler from Simplified Organization explains it like this: "Organizing is not about making things cute or all matching. It is about removing barriers between the person and the task they need to complete." Organizing is about the systems we use to get things done most easily.

That is what this chapter is about. Let's start with the spaces where we homeschool.

ALL THAT STUFF

Some families decide they want a decorated and dedicated school space while others reject a formal space and simply school where they are, integrating their school work into their family space. Neither of these is right or wrong; choose which one is best for your family and what you can do within the limitations of your home.

However you choose to school, the fact remains that homeschooling comes with stuff. There are books, student books, teacher's manuals, office supplies, math manipulatives, games, art supplies, and paper. Oh my! The paper—I can count nine distinct types and sizes of paper within arm's reach of me right now, and I'm not even including the used paper of the kids' completed work and artwork, which is a problem unto itself (see Chapter 10). You've got to have a place to store stuff. This could be an entire room, a closet, a bookshelf, or even a few baskets, boxes, and bins stored in your living room or dining room.

When possible, put items that are frequently used at arm's reach and eye level. If kids will be getting their own supplies, put those items down low so you are not constantly being asked to retrieve something (and so you aren't the only one tall enough to put something away). Utilize baskets, bins, and containers to keep things neat and at hand, and don't be afraid to repurpose items to better meet your needs. I keep all of my thin paperback books in black plastic magazine holders. My husband had tons of them from his magazine collecting days, and they are the perfect way to neatly group and store our picture books to keep them from sliding all over the shelves. I have them labeled by topic, so it is easy for me to grab one and place it on the table to look for a specific book.

Consider reserving a special location for the current year's books and supplies that is separate from the rest. All of my teaching manuals and file folders for the current year, along with the "for mom's hands only" office supplies are kept in a desktop organizer. I love having everything I need on hand and in one spot. Before I had the desk organizer I kept all of my files and books in a file crate on the floor. A nearby shelf or two with a file box would also work. The important thing is to keep the things you use the most close to you, so you don't have to go digging for them every day.

Give each student their own area for their books. I use the oversized cardboard magazine holders for the kids' books. Mostly because this keeps all of it from sliding around and spilling off the shelves. They each have a cubby close to their chair with their magazine holder and anything too large to fit inside. When I tell them to grab their handwriting or Latin workbook, they know exactly where to go to get it and where it should be returned when they are done. They also have their own drawer. I got tired of their projects, crafts, and extra papers littering the top of the school table all the time. Now, I just tuck anything I find into their drawer, and I am much happier. We have a drawer clean-out a number of times each year to keep it under control. If you don't have the extra drawer space where you homeschool, a 12x12 scrapbook paper organizer from your local craft store would also work well and stack easily on a shelf. Just get one for each child.

We also have a dedicated shelf for the books on the family booklist for the year and for our Morning Time basket. These might include read-aloud selections or content-area books for history or science. If it is on a booklist for this year, then it goes on that shelf. When I am ready for a book, I know exactly where it is. If you don't have enough shelf space to dedicate one to each student and the current year's materials, then baskets, plastic containers, and file crates work just as well and can be stored in a closet or under a bed.

ORGANIZING BOOKS AND RESOURCES

Keeping books and curriculum resources tidy on shelves and in boxes is only one part of the battle. The other, perhaps bigger, part is keeping track of what you have. This is to keep you from buying multiple copies of materials but also to help you to remember that you have resources so you use them in your plans and in your school day.

There are a couple of options for book programs that allow you to enter and track your library—from a simple online spreadsheet to apps and barcode readers like LibraryThing or Goodreads. These tools enable you to take your booklists on the go and avoid duplicate purchases or organize your books with tags and keywords to easily check to see which books you have on particular subjects.

Games, manipulatives, and other resources can also be added to a spreadsheet program, or you can add photos of the resource to a photo library on your phone. This will allow you to flip through your personal catalog of resources—either at home or on the go—and organize them by tag and keyword as well. The same tactic can be used for PDFs and digital resources. Simply snap a screenshot of the cover of each PDF and add it to your photo program for an instant visual library.

ORGANIZING PAGES AND PAPERS

If there is one universal truth to homeschooling, it is the fact that we are all drowning in paper. It is everywhere and will soon overrun your home if systems are not put in place to control it. In addition, you can manipulate paper to make it easier to use, helping the flow of your day. Let me explain. Most homeschool materials come in the form of workbooks or digital downloads. For the most part, I don't like using the workbook materials in book form. The stiff bindings that make writing difficult and the cumbersome flipping of pages are two reasons I like to remove pages from workbooks whenever I can. If you have a lefty, binding on a student workbook can make his or her life miserable. I have been known to have the binding cut from a book to eliminate these problems. Your local print shop or office supply shop will do that and drill three holes for you for a couple of bucks.

If you decide to go the loose-leaf route, simply place the pages from each workbook into its own folder and keep it in a file cabinet or crate. Make one folder for each SUBJECT. In those folders store any printouts for that subject. I collate mine (if I have three kids doing the activity, there are three copies of each page, then three of the next, then three of the next, and so on) so that I can reach in and quickly grab exactly what I need. I do the same with perforated workbooks. I don't bother to tear them apart in advance—I just slide the entire workbook into the file.

I encourage you to take the time at the beginning of a term to make at least one term's worth of copies, printouts, etc. for all of the tasks on your procedure lists. This way everything is ready to go for the year, and you won't have to take time during busy school days to get prepped. Remember, because these materials are stored together in a subject folder and undated, you are creating a flexible system that won't make you feel behind.

Each afternoon I grab all the papers from each folder that my student will need for the next day. I put those papers on a clipboard dedicated to that student. This system works for me. It only takes me a few minutes in the evening to grab what we need for the next day. One of the things I love most about this system is that I evaluate my kids' progress every evening. If someone struggled with math, I make a decision that same evening that they need extra practice and pull out another sheet on the same topic. That said, if you are the kind of person who isn't going to load those clipboards every night (not wrong, just a different working style) then you may want to consider a system wherein you load student work weekly instead of daily.

You can do this by purchasing a folder with pockets. Sometimes you can even find soft folders with multiple pockets or use a thin three-ring binder with a pocket divider for each day. At the beginning of the week, simply fill the binder with everything you expect to do for the following week. I suggest you keep an empty folder at the end in which to put items that will eventually get bumped to the following week, and remain flexible in your thinking as life happens and your neatly sorted papers don't stay that way. At the end of the week, take what got bumped and move it back into the pockets for the upcoming week.

There are a variety of organizing systems online, so a little searching will provide you with ideas for a file crate system, workboxes, and a million different variations of each of those systems. Three of the most important considerations when choosing a system for student work are that you choose something that works for your family, your budget, and your space.

The single most important thing in choosing a system, though, just as in choosing a curriculum, is to not forget the person in front of you. While it is appealing for me to have all of my student's work assigned in August for each week of the school year and neatly filed into labeled folders, that system doesn't take into account the interruptions of life and the pace at which my student may or may not master material. If I do all the work to set that up, I have to ask myself if I am willing to abandon it when my child doesn't learn according to my plan. If my goal is to educate and not to just get through curriculum or check boxes, then I must be sure I choose an organization method flexible enough to meet the needs of my child.

THE HOMESCHOOL PLANNER

You will want to have a central location to store all of your important teacher papers and keep track of your lessons. These might include your big-picture planning forms from completing this workbook, as well as your attendance record, grade sheets (if required), completed planning forms, schedules, procedure lists, and lesson plan lists. You can keep a print or digital copy and how you choose to bind this is up to you, but you probably want to have this no more than two to three steps or clicks away. Trust me, if you don't keep this handy there is a good chance you will never mark attendance, you will forget half of your new procedures, and music appreciation will be left off the schedule more than you remember to put it on the schedule.

THE BEST HOMESCHOOL PLANNER FOR YOUR PERSONALITY TYPE

Mystie Winckler

HAVE YOU EVER TRIED YOUR FRIEND'S FAVORITE homeschool planner or planning method, and it was a total flop for you? It's not because there's something wrong with you. More likely, it was a process or a planner that just wasn't a good fit for the way your brain works.

Personality typing á la Myers-Briggs is an attempt to describe different ways our brains are wired: what sort of information we prioritize and how we prefer to make decisions. Our personality type certainly affects the kind of planner that works for us.

After all, we all know different planners and different planning methods work for different people. However, that doesn't mean you have to go through trial and error with every method yourself to find a perfect fit. When you know your personality, you can zone in on what's most likely to work for you, and you can also have more clarity and insight about how to customize your homeschool planner to work for you.

If you don't know your Myers-Briggs personality type, take the test at 16Personalities.com. Based on my research about personality types, applying it to our real lives as homeschooling moms is a useful starting point for not only finding the right homeschool planner for your personality but working your homeschool planner in the most effective way for your type.

ISTJ

THE RESPONSIBLE HOMESCHOOL MOM

The ISTJ homeschool mom has a strong desire to do the right thing and keep track of the details. She will want a record-keeping system and a structured plan. Her planning strength is her reliability and consistency. She needs a traditional school planner with lessons laid out in a way that feels familiar to her. She will want to see the structure of her curriculum as well as her day and be able to mark off visible progress. Digital archiving might appeal to her desire to keep memories without keeping clutter.

ESTJ

THE DOWN-TO-EARTH HOMESCHOOL MOM

The ESTJ homeschool mom is practical, realistic, and driven. She doesn't like to get off course or off topic, and she always has a goal she wants to achieve. The ESTJ is a natural planner and will know what she likes in a planner, be it digital or paper. She needs to beware of overplanning or overloading the schedule and also wary of letting the plan become the master rather than the tool. Including her purpose for homeschooling on her planner where she can see it often will be beneficial.

ISFJ

THE NURTURING HOMESCHOOL MOM

The ISFJ homeschool mom is supportive and nurturing, always seeing what each individual needs in the given moment and doing her best to give it. Because she prefers a supportive role but is good with details, an ISFJ is better at implementing someone else's plan than creating one herself. She needs to find a trusted source for a plan and remember she can adapt it to fit her kids' (and her own) needs. She will prefer a clear-cut plan rather than a loose big-picture concept.

ESFJ

THE COMPANIONABLE HOMESCHOOL MOM

The ESFJ homeschool mom loves the all-together lifestyle homeschooling provides and wants to take advantage of teachable moments and relationship building. An ESFJ will likely love to plan, particularly on paper with a creative flair. She will need a way to juggle the details of her active attention and schedule. A routine flowchart or loop schedule will help her balance working toward goals and taking advantage of the in-the-moment opportunities she sees.

ESTP

THE ADVENTUROUS HOMESCHOOL MOM

An ESTP homeschool mom is enthusiastic about learning and loves to provide interest-based learning, experiences, and projects. She will ensure her children never think learning is boring. An ESTP will prefer to have overarching topics or themes and leave room for exploring resources and experiences and projects. Using a planner to fill in such learning after the fact will work better than trying to plan it out beforehand. Evaluating the progress and current needs every month or term will help an ESTP keep on track and fill in the gaps.

ISTP

THE DIY HOMESCHOOL MOM

The ISTP homeschool mom is less authoritarian and naturally flexible. She won't mind dirty kids or messy science experiments. She loves to see her children explore the natural world. The ISTP might want to try planning alongside each child, taking into account their interests and ideas about structure. Because she's less assertive, getting the kids on board with the learning process will be crucial. She will need a planner that leaves room for acknowledging self-direction and project-based learning.

ESFP

THE IN-THE-MOMENT HOMESCHOOL MOM

The ESFP homeschool mom is friendly, outgoing, and attentive. She can set up beautiful learning environments or experiences (like poetry teas or art centers) naturally and flawlessly. An ESFP will need help creating a plan. She will do best with a ready-to-go plan from a trusted source that leaves plenty of free time and also wiggle room for outside activities and spontaneity. A pen-and-paper approach with short daily lists for the essentials only will most likely serve her best.

ISFP

THE GENEROUS HOMESCHOOL MOM

The ISFP is quiet yet responsive, enjoying a learning lifestyle with her kids without being overbearing. An ISFP will need her routines spelled out in her plans, yet have room in the day for taking advantage of teachable moments and projects. The style of her planner will matter—she should make sure it visually appeals to her.

INFJ

THE UNDERSTANDING HOMESCHOOL MOM

The INFJ homeschool mom listens well and is committed to her vision of a harmonious lifestyle full of love and understanding. Although she's easily overwhelmed with details, she craves structured routine. An INFJ needs to make sure her ideas get out of her head onto paper so she can think through what needs to be done with less overwhelming perfectionism. Having a big-picture plan she can adapt on a daily or weekly basis will likely work well for her.

ENFP

THE CREATIVE HOMESCHOOL MOM

The ENFP homeschool mom loves to say yes to fun—and often has a hard time with the mundane details of life at home. She is easily distracted. An ENFP needs a clearly written plan to help her stay on track, but it needs to be full of variety and allow room for adaptation and flexibility. Her homeschool planner will not be stark or utilitarian, but creative, full, and connected to her vision. It might look like it's all over the place to another type, but because that's how her brain works, it will work for her.

INFP

THE TUNED-IN HOMESCHOOL MOM

The INFP homeschool mom is perceptive, understanding, and sensitive. She will keep a peaceful atmosphere and a deep connection with her children. An INFP will avoid decision-making and be easily overwhelmed, so she needs a planning mentor, whether in person or online, to help her stay on track. She might be drawn to adopting a technologically savvy homeschool planner, but she should avoid any planner that offers too many options or is visually cluttered.

ENFJ

THE ENTHUSIASTIC HOMESCHOOL MOM

The ENFJ homeschool mom loves to connect with her children and big ideas. The more often she can connect her children to big ideas, the happier she will be. An ENFJ will need to make her planner personal and flexible. She will love to adapt based on each child's current needs. Having a big picture that she applies and adapts daily will feel best to her. Leaving space and time to journal about the day in the evening will help her connect reality to her ideals.

INTJ
THE DETERMINED HOMESCHOOL MOM

The INTJ homeschool mom will have her own (highly-researched, well-thought-out) way of doing whatever she sets her mind to. Planning, for her, is the easy and fun part; doing the plan each and every day is draining and difficult. An INTJ desires the most effective homeschool planner, so she will customize either a paper or digital (or combo) solution to fit exactly what she wants. It will be focused on her priorities and have zero fluff. Planning incrementally rather than all at once is a good way for her to keep perspective and enjoyment in the process.

ENTJ
THE DECISIVE HOMESCHOOL MOM

The ENTJ does not believe in impossible once she's decided to do something. She makes things happen, always in line with her guiding principles. An ENTJ will have a streamlined, effective, thorough planning system. She needs to remember to take time to pause regularly and evaluate the situation so she's making appropriate decisions and not letting her grand plan railroad everyone else.

ENTP
THE UNCONVENTIONAL HOMESCHOOL MOM

The ENTP homeschool mom has confidence and energy to spare; she will model and expect independence and unconventional approaches. She is good at seizing opportunities, but not good about following through on details. An ENTP needs a firm conviction about her purpose and goal so that she can improvise in the day-to-day. It might look random and disjointed to others, but if she stays true to her core mission, she'll stay on target. Having a set of big-picture, weekly, or monthly goals rather than detail specifics, then tracking their actual work according to those goals after the fact will help her stay on track while winging it.

INTP
THE INTELLECTUAL HOMESCHOOL MOM

The INTP values her own knowledge base, ensuring it's wide and deep. She finds ideas fascinating and loves to follow rabbit trails and work out theories. An INTP's homeschool planner is simple: it's a book list. Read books. Discuss. Because she has a hard time with physical details, she needs to think more about giving her things and books convenient homes than about keeping a homeschool planner. A simple, unfussy, flexible bullet journal will serve her purposes nicely.

PROS AND CONS OF VARIOUS PLANNERS

After reading Mystie's description of planners for your personality type, you might be considering various kinds of homeschool planners. Here are a number of available options and the pros and cons for each type.

- The Pre-Printed Homeschool Planner
- The Print-It-Yourself Homeschool Planner
- The Online Homeschool Planner
- The Bullet Journal Homeschool Planner

THE PRE-PRINTED HOMESCHOOL PLANNER

These attractive spiral-bound planners are often what homeschoolers first consider when they think about a homeschool planner. They are available at your favorite bookstore or website along with various custom options from printers online. Some homeschoolers even prefer adapting a printed planner designed for a classroom teacher as their planner.

 PROS

 CONS

PROS	CONS
• There are a wide variety of beautiful, professional designs available along with fun stickers and accessories.	• You are limited by the available forms in the planner. There may be some forms you have no desire to use, and there may not be forms for all your planning needs. You will not be able to add additional pages unless the binding allows for that (discbound).
• Most include monthly calendars as well as weekly planning spreads.	
• Most include a record-keeping section for attendance and grades.	• Most pre-printed homeschool planners are date- and grid-dependent which limits flexibility in homeschool planning and often causes stress.
• They often include a handy pocket or two.	• Must be purchased every year.
	• You must write in the planner by hand since it's pre-printed.

THE PRINT-IT-YOURSELF HOMESCHOOL PLANNER

Since this workbook comes with optional access to a print-yourself planner, you can tell this is obviously the planner I prefer. Print-it-yourself options are available for free or a small fee online. You want to look for a planner that has the option of filling in the forms digitally for the ultimate in flexibility.

 PROS

 CONS

- There are a wide variety of designs available to fit any style.
- Can be purchased once and reused year after year.
- You can choose which forms you want to include in your planner and not print the ones you won't use.
- Forms you can complete digitally do not have to be printed at all and can be accessed via a tablet or computer for a paperless planner option.
- Digital forms can be saved, updated, and reused in the future, cutting down on work.
- You can choose to either type in forms for speed and convenience or go old-school and put pen to paper if you think better that way.

- You are limited by the available forms in each set, and there may not be forms for all your planning needs, causing you to need to create some forms of your own.
- The cost of printing (and binding if you choose to do so) can make this option more costly than a pre-printed planner.

THE ONLINE HOMESCHOOL PLANNER

For those who want to go completely digital, online and app-based planning systems offer advantages that other systems do not.

 PROS

 CONS

PROS

- Plans can often be copied and reused for other years and other students. Some planners even allow users to access a database of pre-planned lessons for popular resources.
- To-do lists are easily created and shared with older students through their own electronic devices and versions of the app.
- Many online planners have developed systems that allow parents to migrate unfinished lessons to a new day, thereby shifting future lessons forward as well.

CONS

- These planners rarely have an attractive user interface. If you want something pretty, you likely won't find much choice here.
- If your planner does not allow for lesson migration, the system can be stress-inducing and time-consuming to adjust as life happens.
- Logging in to check on lesson plans can be a distraction from school.
- Setting up these planners often requires the learning curve of new software and the up-front work of entering lessons.
- Some people will miss the pen-to-paper aspect that might help their thinking and planning.

Note: Some homeschoolers have begun to adapt online productivity tools like Trello and Asana for their homeschool planning and assigning lessons to students. If you are a techy homeschooler, these options can be a valuable addition to your homeschool planning arsenal.

THE BULLET JOURNAL HOMESCHOOL PLANNER

Eschewing printed forms and technology altogether, the bullet journal homeschool planner embodies the ultimate in flexibility for homeschool moms. You simply grab a blank notebook (or cheap spiral notebook) and some pens and get started. For an introduction to the original bullet journal system, check out the website bulletjournal.com.

 PROS

 CONS

- The system is incredibly flexible. You can write in your vision, goals, lists, weekly plans, etc. If you don't like the way a page is working, simply turn to the next blank page and start again.
- Your bullet journal can be as creative and beautiful or as simple as you want it to be.
- The journal provides a ton of space for recording learning after the fact. Jot a few notes or create narrative entries of the week's learning. The choice is up to you.

- Some might be frustrated or stymied by the lack of structure.
- There is a danger in gettings so caught up in the creation of pages that very little concrete planning (or homeschooling) gets done.
- A good organizational system is needed for those families who are required to put together portfolios at the end of the school year. Make sure to set up an index to be able to find the information you need easily.

WHAT TO KEEP IN YOUR PLANNER OR BINDER

It's helpful to keep all of your homeschool paperwork in one location and right at your fingertips. To that end, most moms keep a homeschool binder of sorts for storing these items. Here are some things you might find helpful to put in your binder:

- **Long-term planning forms:** any and all of the forms have a place in your binder. including your vision statement, goals, resource lists, long-term calendars, and wish lists for future homeschool ideas.

- **Copies of schedules and routines:** yearly, term, loop, weekly, and daily

- **Calendars:** year-at-a-glance and monthly school calendar

- **Lesson plans:** simple and detailed lesson plan lists and procedure lists

- **Booklists:** for books you plan to read as well as a blank one for each student and for the family, to record other selections you read.

- **Attendance forms**

- **Legal paperwork:** copies of letters of intent, state standards, and other forms

- **Homeschool requirements:** if you have specific requirements you need to meet for your state, keep a copy handy.

- **Grade reporting and transcript planning for high school**

- **Review form:** for your periodic plan review (see Chapter 10)

- **Notes and journal pages:** use a notes page to record accomplishments and concerns about each student throughout the year.

COMPLETED STUDENT WORK

For those loose papers that are complete, you can do one of two things—store them in a folder or binder, or throw them away/recycle them. Yep, I said that. Whatever you decide to keep or toss, a couple of factors should come into your decision-making process. If you live in a state that requires portfolio evaluation, you will want to evaluate and choose carefully which items to keep, making sure you provide any samples your state may require. Even if your state does not require a portfolio, it is a good educational practice to keep a record of your students' progress in case you are ever asked by a legal entity to provide one; it is also personally useful to go through the reflection process creating a portfolio requires. It's fun to look back on how far a student has progressed, and seeing old work can increase a student's confidence in their own abilities.

While these are far from definitive, here are few suggestions to help you decide what to keep.

- **Math:** Keep a selection of chapter or unit tests. If you do not use math tests, then a few samples of student work will suffice. You can be selective. There is no need to keep samples of the student's ability to do single-digit addition when you have a sample of them successfully completing multiple-digit addition with regrouping. Math skills build on one another, so limit yearly samples to a handful that show the farthest progression in mastery.

- **Writing samples:** I tend to err on the side of too many when it comes to writing samples. At the very least, be sure to keep one from the beginning of the year and one from the end to show progression. I would also keep any that are especially well-done.

- **Handwriting:** One sample of the student's best work from the beginning and end of the year will suffice.

- **Content area subjects:** Keep anything the student especially enjoyed or was interested in. I would start by asking them what some of their favorite assignments were. Other than that, keep a sample or two that demonstrates writing skills or student interaction with (as opposed to regurgitation of) the material. In other words, throw away any multiple choice tests or worksheets and keep the diary entry the student wrote about being a Pilgrim child at the first Thanksgiving.

- **Art:** No advice here. I am a sucker for my kids' artwork and have the full Rubbermaid containers to prove it. I am trying to be better. I do recommend snapping pictures of three-dimensional projects and getting them out of the house quickly!

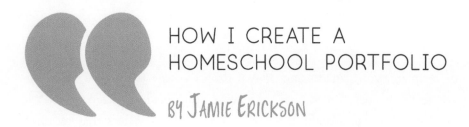

HOW I CREATE A HOMESCHOOL PORTFOLIO

by Jamie Erickson

THROUGHOUT THE YEAR, I stash away potential work in accordion-style folders. The sections and tabs help me to organize the work from day to day so that I don't face a mountain of papers to sort at the end of the year. It acts as my first line of defense against hoarding. Since I color-code our school day, I keep a different colored folder for each child. If my kids complete a project that I think could potentially make the final cut for their portfolio, I toss it into their folder for safekeeping until May.

When the school year ends and the accordion files are bulging and ready to be emptied, it's time to actually create the portfolio. With files in one hand and finished workbooks in the other, I begin to sort through math sheets, creative writing assignments, handwriting practice pages, and the like. Obviously, not everything will be worth keeping. Some of it was just useful in the moment. It's up to me to separate the good from the best.

As I sort, I select three work samples from each subject. For objective subjects like math and language, I pick one sample from the beginning of the year, one from the middle of the year, and one from the end of the year. For subjective subjects like creative writing and art, I'm more purposeful in my selection and save work that was particularly important or that sufficiently shows my child's progress from the beginning of the year to the end of it.

After I've selected samples from every single subject, I toss all the rest of the work. (If it's not worthy of the portfolio, it's not worthy of prime shelf space in my house.) Then, I format my portfolio. I use a three-ring binder with divider tabs, but a file folder, plastic bin, or banker's box would work just as well. Long ago, I had hoped to make separate binders for each one of my children every year, but since I now homeschool five kids, I don't have the time or the space to make so many. Plus, because so much of our learning is done together as a group, it's difficult and redundant to compile it individually.

Before inserting all the work samples that I've gathered, I create divider tabs within the binder to separate each child's papers from the others'. I divide the binder using the following sub-headings:

GROUP BIBLIOGRAPHY

This section contains the information for any subject or project we completed together as a family, such as Bible, history, science, or art. Within this section, I insert the following:

- A bibliography page listing the subjects we have done together as a group and every book we used for those subjects. Since our history curriculum consists of dozens and dozens of living books, I just note the bibliography info of the curriculum guide on the main bibliography page and then list the book titles on a separate sheet of paper. I keep a running list of these historical books all year long in my computer, print it off in the spring, and add it to the binder.

- A photocopy of the table of contents page of any encyclopedic/spine-type books we read from for our group subjects. If we did not read through the entire book but hopped around to the portions that applied to certain units, I highlight the sections we completed in order to show which areas of study we focused on and which ones we skipped.

- A list of all the read-alouds we enjoyed together that year. Again, I keep a running list on my computer all year long so I can just print it out when I'm compiling the portfolio.

FIELD TRIPS

Since so much of our learning happens on the go, I always create a field trip section in our portfolio. It includes the following:

- A list of all the places we visited. I make a note of the date as well as a few specific points of interest we saw or experienced while we were there. I keep this running list on my computer and print it out at the end of the year.

- A clear plastic sleeve filled with any ticket stubs, brochures, and printables from the field trip locations as proof of our visit.

- Photo sleeves or digital files on CD to display pictures of our field trips.

SPECIAL PROJECTS

Since I have a large age span of kids, I don't often assign them projects together. But when I do, I include the following information in the portfolio:

- A list of all non-book, non-worksheet-related learning such as YouTube videos we watched, audio programs we listened to, science projects we completed, etc. I make sure to record the date the project was completed and a short description (3-4 words) of what it entailed.

- Photo sleeves or a CD of pictures of our completed projects. Due to lack of space, we cannot keep all the large crafts and displays, but the pictures help us retain the memory of them.

HOMESCHOOL CO-OP

Much of our enrichment learning happens at our co-op. Here's what I save and display in this section of our binder:

- A hard copy of our co-op schedule that lists our basic units of study/book club lists for the year.

- If we happen to do a group skit or performance at the end-of-the-year spring program, I include a copy of the script.

- Photographs or a photo CD of co-op pictures from the year.

SAMPLE WORK

After I've compiled all of our group work in the previous binder sections, I then create separate tabs for each of my kids. These sections will be used to display samplings from their individual core subjects like math, language arts, writing, etc. Within each child's section, I include the following:

- A bibliography page for the books he/she used for core subjects.

- A copy of the table of contents of encyclopedic/spine-type books that each child read only portions from. I highlight the sections that he/she read.

- Three individual work samples from each subject. These are the worksheets I previously culled from their workbooks or accordion files.

- A clear plastic sleeve to hold any awards/certificates that he/she earned throughout the year from church, piano lessons, community sports, county fair, etc.

PROJECT PACKS

- Some of the save-worthy projects like lapbooks, journals, or minibooks are awkwardly shaped, are too large for the three-ring binder, or are too delicate to be three-hole punched. Instead, these get placed inside large manila envelopes that get tucked behind the appropriate child's binder tab.

- Before stashing the completed binder in the basement with all the previous years' portfolios, I label the spine with the school year and the initials and "grade levels" of each of the kids included.

OTHER ITEMS TO INCLUDE IN A PORTFOLIO

- Report cards/high school credit
- Medical/immunization records
- Apprenticeship hour logs
- Annual achievement test scores
- Extracurricular logs
- Leadership/volunteer logs
- Certifications/training received
- Employment experiences

GRADING PAPERS

I know a number of you have older kids who need grades assigned or you are required to grade papers by the state. Regardless, our kids need feedback on the work that they are doing. Here are a few tips for dealing with papers that need to be graded.

PROVIDE IMMEDIATE FEEDBACK WHENEVER POSSIBLE.

I always check the math page before I let anyone be done for the day (they just leave it lying open near my seat until I can grab the teacher's manual and look it over). This way they immediately have to correct their mistakes. This works the same with spelling, grammar, etc. The immediate correction is good for them, I know before I plan for the following day if they are ready to move to the next lesson or need more practice, and nothing piles up. You can't evaluate if your child needs to do every lesson if you aren't checking work daily. If they need extra practice, don't move them on. Likewise, if they really don't need extra practice, don't torture them by making them spend time on something that bores them.

HAVE THEM GRADE THEIR OWN PAPERS.

Once a child reaches about ten years old, they can check their own spelling, grammar worksheet, or math page. Have them grab the manual and circle any items they missed. They can do this while in the same room as you. (Tip: don't give them the manual and send them off to do the work and grade their own papers. Ahem.) Then they should correct their mistakes and "meet" with you for a minute to discuss any issues. Remember, issuing a grade is about improving skills and knowledge, not catching someone in what they don't know. Let them be part of the process.

SCHEDULE A DEDICATED TIME TO GRADE.

When you have to grade things that take longer and need more in-depth feedback—like a writing assignment or project—then set aside time once a week to get that done. Choose a time that works for you (It might not be Friday afternoon, right?) and do not let the work pile up—*this is the key.* If you are following strategies 1 and 2 above, your stack should be smaller and more manageable.

Action Items

1. Choose and tidy up your school space. Shop your home or make a shopping list of items you need to set up your space. Get your current books, resources, and curricula in a handy location.

2. Set up spaces for your kids' books for the current year.

3. Determine how you will organize your papers. Print copies for the next term (or year), cut bindings from books, set up your filing system.

4. Start cataloging your books and resources so you know what you have. This does not have to be done all at one time; it can be tackled in small chunks over a few months.

5. Set up a system for completed work and make any related purchases (binders, containers).

6. Set aside time on your calendar for grading.

7. Remember that you have to live with any system for a while before you can evaluate it properly. Don't be afraid to change and adapt as the year goes on and you see what is and is not working.

CHAPTER 9

PUTTING IT ALL TOGETHER

At this point you likely have a number of different forms, lesson plan lists, procedure lists, and so on. You have books, curriculum, and a homeschool planner. You have a vision and goals. Yet you might be wondering how to make all of these different pieces work together. How do you go from plans on paper (or on screen) to actually living out your homeschool from day to day? This chapter will show you how.

COMMUNICATING PLANS TO YOUR KIDS

Somehow you have to get all of the materials you have prepped and planned TO the students for them to complete. You have to communicate with them what the assignments are and what you expect from them each day. You have to have a way to pass over those materials you have taken the time to print and store. And as the kids get older, you want them to use the systems you create to begin to work independently.

Different families will use different methods from high-tech apps to color-coded bins, or pens and a weekly grid. My favorite, though, is far simpler than all of those.

COMMUNICATION METHOD: SPIRAL NOTEBOOKS

Yep, plain old spiral notebooks. I have found nothing more flexible for communicating assignments than these. They DO take a few minutes to complete each day, but honestly, I spend less than five minutes per child once my plan is in place.

HOW I'M USING SPIRAL NOTEBOOKS TO SIMPLIFY HOMESCHOOLING

BY SARAH MACKENZIE

EARLY IN DECEMBER, I WAS AT CHURCH, trying to keep my mind focused—it kept drifting off to schoolwork. In my head, I was finagling how we could possibly combine subjects or weed something out and do less in order to make the school day work. The days were difficult. Even though I had pared back and simplified as much as possible, we were still struggling to hit those most important subjects. Twin toddlers change everything! Add a two-year-old to the mix and things can get downright disastrous by 10 a.m., let me tell you. Our school day was feeling it.

After church, I moseyed out to the foyer and gave my friend Sheila a big hug. "How's it going?" she asked with a smile. Sheila homeschooled her three kids into adulthood, and they are some of the most fantastic kids you'll ever meet. Sheila is not so far removed that she forgets how hard it was, but she's got this end-of-the-homeschooling-road wisdom and insight that I crave to learn from. I absolutely adore her. She asked that simple question, and I started to fall apart, saying things like, "I can't do this! There's too much to get to! Maybe what I'm trying to do here IS actually impossible?" Sheila listened (like she always does), and then she said, "Well, how much of their schoolwork are they doing on their own?" I stopped to think. She followed up, "And how are you giving them assignments?"

Right. That. I write them on a whiteboard each morning when I finally get around to it, which is usually in between grabbing one twin off the dining room table and the other one out of the kitchen garbage and washing Posy's jelly face and changing a diaper and scolding someone for forgetting to shut the door to the basement where a toddler nearly plummeted to his demise. It's not a good system.

Sheila came over the next day. She told me I would need a simple 10-cent spiral notebook for each kid, and she would show me what to do. And she did. Here's the groundbreaking system. Are your ready for this? Each evening, I write down the kids' assignments for the next day in their own assignment book. What? You thought I was going to say something grand and amazing, and you're a little let down? I know. I was skeptical at first, too, but I have been floored at the change this simple method has made in our homeschool.

See, after I employed this notebook system, we began to consistently get to pretty much everything I assigned for each day by early in the afternoon. For the first time, I wasn't having to wrack my brain to remember what we were supposed to do when. Each morning after breakfast, the big kids do their one morning chore, dress and brush their teeth, and then they set to work on their school notebooks. Instead of feeling pulled between teaching a lesson, caring for toddlers, and making soup for dinner, I go about my business with the little ones, and the big kids go about theirs.

When they have a question or need help with an assignment, they bring their materials to me wherever I am, and I help them on the spot. If someone else is getting help at the moment, they work on something else in their notebook until I'm free. I know what you're thinking (I was thinking the same thing). Something like this, right?

"I don't have time to write down assignments each night."

The truth is, it takes 10 to 15 minutes. I spent a little time making a master spreadsheet of assignments and how frequently I want each thing tackled, and I use that as a quick reference. It literally takes me 10 minutes (max) to look at the spreadsheet and write down the assignments for all three of my school-agers. If I really can't carve out 10 minutes to do this, I skip sweeping the floor, folding the laundry, or checking Facebook, and I do this instead. It's worth it.

"Why should I write it out when I could just print out a checklist?"

Because something about the act of writing it out by hand triggers the brain to engage. When I'm writing out my thirteen-year-old's assignments, I can tell I'm giving her too much work if it's taking me a while to write or the paper is filling up. It's so easy to just pop in one more assignment on a spreadsheet on your computer. It's harder to make the space when you're writing it out by hand.

Also, writing it out means I'm constantly in touch with where each child is in each of his or her subjects. Instead of just giving an assignment that says "Do the next math assignment," it says "Do Lesson 14." See that box before the math assignment? That's what this child checks off when she's done. The box after the assignment means I need to check it off for her to really be "done" for the day. If she made a lot of errors, the next day's assignment will likely be "Watch lesson 14 one more time and make corrections to yesterday's assignment."

Writing each assignment out by hand means I'm staying connected with where she is in every subject. I can tell if a Latin assignment is taking her longer than usual, or if she's flying through it in her sleep. In fact, I can more easily keep my finger on the pulse of where all of my kids are in their different subjects.

Some tips that help to make this work:

Resist the urge to make this more complicated than it needs to be. I use colored pens, but it's just for fun, not for color coding. You want to remove as many barriers as possible to making this tool do the thing it's supposed to do. Simple is always better.

Keep the notebooks handy. Ours go in a basket on our kitchen counter. The kids take them out, use them, and put them back. They don't disappear into the school bins or backpacks or any such nonsense. They need to be handy, visible, and always in the same place.

Use the last ten pages or so for a booklist. Have you been meaning to print out a booklist form for your kids to record their personal reading this year? Me too. Why I can't ever manage to keep enough of those around (or keep track of them when I do) is beyond me, but it's always the case. I put a Post-it flag marking the last 10 or so pages of the spiral notebook, and the kids have been instructed to write the book title, author, and number of pages of each book they read on their own. At the end of the year, I'll make transcribing this onto the computer a keyboarding assignment for one of my young typists.

So if you're feeling a bit in-over-your-head as you hit the books once again, grab a spiral notebook and see if this super-simple system might see you through the dark winter months.

It has been transformative for us, really helping me to teach from rest and restoring my peace in our schooling. The kids love it too, and have thanked me multiple times for organizing their school day this way.

Here is why spiral notebooks work. First, you are writing assignments for the school day the night before. By that time you typically have a good idea of what your schedule is going to be for the day you are planning. The only thing that can mess you up is if something goes off the rails that morning—and then you just save the plan for the following day.

Second, these lists are so flexible to changes. Strike through the date at the top and write a new one, cross a couple of things off the list and move them to the next day. Nothing is set in stone here—it is the ultimate in flexibility. You also make decisions in the moment about what your kid needs. Are they still struggling with that math concept? Schedule another review sheet for the next day. Did they get it on the first go? Move on to something else the next day. Did they melt down during spelling? Just stop. You won't be behind. Put the rest of the lesson on the list for tomorrow. This is customized learning at its best.

HERE IS WHY SPIRAL NOTEBOOKS WORK

A couple of notes about filling out the notebooks at the end of the day. First, my ambitious self never gets to those notebooks in the morning before school like I think she will. She just isn't that trustworthy, so filling them out at the end of the day is really the best option for me. The other benefit of filling out the notebooks at the end of the day is that tired, end-of-the-school-day mom has much less of a tendency to pile on things than fresher, less-tired morning mom. Filling out the notebooks at the end of the day helps me to keep it real in my homeschool. Finally, your kids know at the beginning of the day what they need to complete in order to be done. This encourages them to work hard because once the list is finished, they are free. Also, the list is the "bad guy" in my house. The youngest might complain about what he has to do, but he typically blames the list and not me.

WHAT ABOUT PRE-READERS?

If you have kids who can't read well or are not terribly independent, you can still make them a list. I did it for my youngest for years. Why? Because, BAM, *I* knew exactly what I was doing with him each day. I didn't have to stop and think about it in the morning—I just followed the list and did what was next. Sure, the list was more for me, but it worked.

FAMILY LISTS

If you do a number of subjects together as a family, you can create a spiral notebook list for your family subjects each day as well. Typically, if a few of my kids work on things together (not everyone), I just write the subject on each of their lists and wait for a time each day when they can work together.

MIDDLE AND HIGH SCHOOL

As your kids get older, it is helpful to give them practice managing their own time. Transition from the daily spiral notebook lists to a weekly grid. This transition will happen at different ages for different kids. Some will want to grab the reins and have freedom over their own schedules while others will wilt under the weight of seeing all of their work laid out for the week. It may take a couple of false starts before you hit on the right time to make this change.

Start by having them plan out one subject for the week on their own and bring that to you to check over. As they gain confidence and ability, turn over more of the assigning to them with periodic checks to be sure they are doing OK. Keep in mind that some kids will gravitate towards working longer blocks on a single subject and getting a week's worth of work done on one day. Non-traditional scheduling is their way of figuring out what works for them.

DISBURSING MATERIALS

Now we have to get these lists and all the workbook pages and copies we have made to the kids so that they can complete them. This isn't the only way, but *my* favorite way to do it is the clipboard. It is quick and easy to load, doesn't take a ton of space, and gets the job done. Each of my kids has a clipboard that hangs on a hook in our schoolroom. On their clipboards we keep curriculum progress charts (the kind that come with stickers), their papers for each day, and their spiral notebooks.

Each day, when I fill out the notebook for the next day, I pull out the papers they need from my file folders and clip them to the clipboard behind their notebook. This accomplishes a couple of things. One, it is a form of lesson planning for me—I only put on the clipboard what I think we will be able to accomplish in one day. Two, it allows the student to see only the work they are required to finish that day (they know when they are done, so there's no continuous asking), and it allows them to self-start in the morning with subjects they are able to work on alone. Since we hang our clipboards on hooks in the schoolroom, the kids can easily reach them each morning. This way, they get what they need when they need it. If we miss a day or two of school, it is all sitting there waiting when we get back.

Here is how the whole process looks at my house:

1. As each child finishes their school work for the day, they check off their list. When they are done, I use a break in my schedule to reboot their notebook and clipboard.

2. Looking at what they completed and thinking about how they did on their lessons, I begin making their list for the next day. At this point I can glance at our calendar and school schedule and think about what tomorrow should look like to know how much to include.

3. I turn to my folders and grab any papers they will need for the next day. Those go on the clipboard behind the list, and it all gets hung on the hook. The entire process takes about five minutes.

TEACHING WITH SCHEDULES AND LISTS

If you have been creating your plan step-by-step through this book, you now likely have a couple of different schedules and also a few different lesson plan or procedure lists. Teaching with these multiple forms is easy. As you start your day, check your schedule first. Are you in a skill work block? Are you starting your day with Morning Time? Maybe you are working on a loop schedule time first. Once you have determined *which* subject or subjects you are doing, then move to your lesson plan list or procedure list to tell you specifically *what* to do. As the year goes on you will consult the schedules and even some of the procedure lists less and less.

My lesson planning doesn't involve daily grids, calendars, or planning pages. Instead, it merely consists of consulting my schedules and my lists, then marking off what we have done at the end of the day.

ACTION ITEMS

① Decide how you will communicate with your students—will it be a weekly planning grid, an app, or a spiral notebook? Purchase what you need to make this happen.

② Decide how you will distribute learning materials to your students. What will you give them each day and how? What will they grab from their shelves?

CHAPTER 10

PLANNING IN ACTION

Some of my favorite things are things that hold infinite promise. A newborn baby. A freshly sharpened No. 2 pencil. A neat and tidy homeschool plan. I joke that I enjoy the planning more than the actual homeschooling because in the planning, nothing goes wrong.

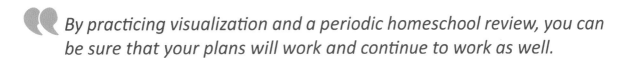 *By practicing visualization and a periodic homeschool review, you can be sure that your plans will work and continue to work as well.*

But life, especially life with kids, is messy and unpredictable. So in order to be sure that our promising plans are going to work and continue to work, we have to be proactive about gauging the success of our plans. Fortunately I have a couple of tools I use to help ensure that the plans I made will be useful and continue to be useful as the year goes on. By practicing visualization and a periodic homeschool review, you can be sure that your plans will work and continue to work as well.

VISUALIZATION AS A HOMESCHOOL HELP

When I was in my twenties, I decided I was going to engage in some fun activities I never got to do as a kid. One of these was to take figure skating lessons. It wasn't long before I was spending hours each week on the ice, learning the intricate ins and outs of skating tricks and ice dances. I even had a dance partner and skated with a synchronized team for a while. I had a fabulous coach who remains a good friend to this day. One of the best things she ever taught me, other than the tango, was to visualize my performances before I stepped out onto the ice. In fact, she didn't just have me picture them in my mind, but go through the mental motions of doing them over and over and over again.

Generally speaking, visualization is the process of creating a mental image or intention of what you want to happen or feel in reality. The great thing about visualizing your homeschool day is that it will help you find kinks or holes in your plan before you even begin homeschooling.

HOW DOES VISUALIZATION WORK?

Find a quiet space where you can sit for a few minutes in silence. (Don't laugh! I know it is hard but it will be worth it, even if you have to do it at midnight.) Ideally, I like to do my visualization while I'm sitting in my chair in the schoolroom. I even go through some of the motions of reaching and grabbing as I visualize (it's my old skating coach's fault, I am sure) but more than once I have discovered something that was missing by going through this process.

I start by checking my daily plan for the first item on our list. Do I have everything I need to complete that item? How do I get everyone to the table? What are they supposed to be doing? Is what they need nearby? Do the links in my PDF work? Can I easily grab the art supplies? Did I put the notebooking pages on the clipboard? Where are their math DVDs? Do they have a place to store the ones that aren't being used? What is this child doing while I am working on reading with this other one?

I mentally work my way through a school day, making sure I have materials, items are prepared, and no big exclamation points popping up to say, "Hey that is never going to work!"

Does this mean everything will be perfect the first day? Heck no! But I can't tell you how many times I have found something I forgot or headed off a problem before it became one by visualizing my way through my plan. Don't skip this step.

An additional method of remembering holes in your plan as you find them is to keep an index card close by as you go through the first few weeks of school. My friend Brandy Vencel suggested this one to me. As you work through the first week of your plans, make note of any problems you discover, missing items, or little issues. This way you can address those in the evening or on the weekend without having to interrupt your school day.

MAKING SURE YOUR PLAN CONTINUES TO WORK

One thing to keep in mind as your family grows and changes, as you enter new seasons of life with a new baby or only teens, or as your views of education change (because after all, we are always learning and growing), you will need to reevaluate your plans and change them accordingly. What works for you this day or this year may not work the next, and the younger your children are, the faster your schedule will need to adapt to their growth and needs. So be sure to reevaluate often—sometimes even mid-school year—and adapt as you go.

SCHEDULE A REVIEW

The first thing you need to do is schedule a regular review period into your homeschool year. If you organized your year in terms, this will be easy. Simply schedule a day during one of your term breaks to hold your review. If you didn't schedule terms, then you will need to choose a day on the calendar. I would suggest at least four times a year or once a quarter. Go ahead and circle those days now and place them in your daily calendar or planner. Set a reminder or do what you normally do to remember a special event is coming.

Try to set aside a day to do your review when you can take the time to dig in and do more planning—this needs to be a big chunk in your calendar. For some folks it will be an afternoon, but others might need a day or two to make adjustments, depending on what their review reveals. If you have decided to prepare and organize your materials by term, then you would get the next term prepared at the same time.

HOLDING THE REVIEW

We have made a handy review checklist for you to use as you review your homeschool every few months. You can use it to guide you in this process.

Start your review by reading over your vision. Ask yourself if there are any changes to make to this document and also ask if you have been living it out. Where might you make adjustments?

Next, pull out the goal sheets for each of your students. Are they meeting these goals? Are you doing the needed behaviors and actions? Are there any you can cross off and update? Do you need to add a new goal to the list?

Do a mental check of your resources and curriculum. In fact, I suggest never allowing yourself to change curriculum until a review period. This ensures that you have actually given the curriculum a fair chance before tossing it. Have you done it consistently enough to be sure there is really a problem with the resource?

If they are struggling, let your kids know when the evaluation date is so they know you will take a look at the curriculum then, but that they must use it until that date. This prevents curriculum hopping that might be unnecessary.

Ask yourself, *Are things working?* Now is a great time to flip through the front matter of your teacher's guides and make note of any tips that are there. So often I forget the helpful information in the front of the teacher's books. Having a set time to review it ensures I am not making using the curriculum harder than it was intended to be.

Next audit your overall, weekly, and daily schedules and routines. Does everything there seem to be working? Are there areas where you are struggling?

This is the time to take stock of things like inconsistencies or your own morning struggles or the fact that your thirteen-year-old is staying up too late each evening, resulting in later starts and grumpy mornings. These things get away from us, and review is a good time to take note and pull them back in.

Are you feeling busy and stressed out? Can you take some steps to feel less busy, or do you need to eliminate an activity from your calendar?

Review your procedures. Are they working? Do they need to be tweaked?

Look at your lesson plan lists and note your progress—catch up any check marks. Is something falling through the cracks each week? How can you adjust to make sure that subject gets done?

Finally, this is the time to prep new materials for the next term and tidy the school area. Throw things away, fix the sloppy spots, and freshen things up.

In order to keep your homeschool plan running smoothly, you must do regular maintenance. That is what will keep you soaring along through the entire school year.

ACTION ITEMS

1. Set aside time to visualize your school day. Walk through the day in your head to be sure you have everything prepared and ready to go.

2. Circle periodic review dates on your calendar and print out enough review checklists for the entire school year. tore them in your teacher's binder.

PERIODIC REVIEW CHECKLIST

☐ Read over your vision again. Are any changes to make to this document? Have you been living this? Where might you make adjustments?

☐ Pull out the goal sheets for each of your students. Are they meeting these goals? Are you doing the needed behaviors and actions? Are there any goals you can cross off and update? Do you need to add a new goal to the list?

☐ Are things working with your curriculum and resources? Now is a great time to flip through the front matter of your teacher's guide and make note of any tips that are there. Have you done it consistently enough to be sure there is really a problem with the resource? Do you need to make changes?

☐ Audit your overall, weekly, and daily schedules and routines. Does everything there seem to be working OK? Are there areas where you are struggling? Are you feeling busy and stressed out? Can you take some steps to feel less busy or do you need to eliminate an activity from your calendar?

☐ Take stock of inconsistency or character issues (the kids and yours). Are there areas that need to be addressed? What plans can you put in place to do that?

☐ Review your procedures. Are they working? Do they need to be tweaked?

☐ Look at your lesson plan lists and note your progress — catch up any check marks. Is something falling through the cracks each week? How can you adjust to make sure that subject gets done?

☐ Prep new materials and make copies for the next term and tidy the school area. Throw things away, fix the sloppy spots, and freshen things up.

AFTERWORD

You've done it! If you have followed all of the action steps in this book, you now have your very own plan for your next homeschool year. I knew you could do it! Most importantly, you have a plan that takes into account your children, your family, and yourself. A plan like this will offer the greatest chance of success—for you, and for your children in their academic journeys.

If you have any questions or concerns, I am always happy to chat more with you. You can find me at pambarnhill.com or by emailing pam@pambarnhill.com. Happy planning!

ACKNOWLEDGMENTS

Taking on a project of this magnitude is not something we can do alone. I would like to thank my husband Matt for his support of all my crazy schemes and his willingness to consume pizza for dinner yet again. My three beautiful children are a daily delight and inspiration behind what I do. Sure, some days they drive me crazy, but there is no place I would rather be than home with them. My good friends Sarah Mackenzie, Mystie Winckler, Dawn Garrett, and Brandy Vencel who so graciously shared their ideas, their talents, and their inspiration to all parts of the process of creating this book; you guys are a blessing to me. My editor Harmony Harkema for her keen eye and fabulous homeschool insights. Melinda Martin, my designer, for always making me look good. A special thank you to the other contributors to this book, whose voices made it even more of a helpful tool for homeschoolers everywhere: Amy Milcic, Shelly Sangrey, and Jamie Erickson. My homeschool tribe provided a sounding board and encouragement throughout the writing process: Jessica Lawton, Julia Feeley, Tara Maple, Mary Reiter, and Michele Tyson. We may be counter-cultural, but we're all in it together.

CONTRIBUTOR BIOS

When she's not curating memories, hoarding vintage books, or playing ringmaster to her own live-in circus of five, JAMIE ERICKSON can be found encouraging and equipping a growing tribe of homeschooling mothers all across the globe through her blog, The Unlikely Homeschool. In her book, *Homeschool Bravely: How to Trust God, Squash Doubt, and Teach Your Child With Confidence*, Jamie reminds the fearful mom that while she may not have an alphabet soup of letters behind her name or the golden seal of the world's approval, she has all she needs to homeschool perfectly.

DAWN GARRETT loves learning with her three children at home. Following the principles of Charlotte Mason, she and her children learn about God and His cosmos by studying the seven liberal arts in order to know Him better, imitate Him and His ways, and share about Him with others. Dawn is one of the curators of the popular @charlottemasonirl community on Instagram, blogs at ladydusk.blogspot.com, and acts as Community Manager for pambarnhill.com. She is the author of *I Am, I Can, I Ought, I Will: Charlotte Mason's Motto Explained for Upper Elementary Students* which can be found free on her blog.

SARAH MACKENZIE is the USA Today bestselling author of *The Read Aloud Family: Make Meaningful and Lasting Connections with Your Kids* and *Teaching from Rest: A Homeschooler's Guide to Unshakable Peace*. Her popular Read-Aloud Revival podcast has been downloaded over 4 million times by families all over the world. She lives in the Northwest with her husband, Andrew, and loves to make sure their kids are well-stocked in the best books she can find. Connect with Sarah at readaloudrevival.com

AMY MILCIC, a homeschool soccer mom to five boys, believes that you can have homeschool fun as you boost learning, relationships, and life. She shares resources and support to help you shine as you rock your homeschool at rockyourhomeschool.com.

SHELLY SANGREY is a Christian wife and mom of 11 great kids, ranging in age from 5 to 25. Finding her niche in the world of relaxed homeschooling, Shelly has made it her mission in life to help other homeschool moms escape the overwhelm, comparison, and insecurities that often accompany taking on a task as important as educating one's own children. You can find her on her blog at redheadmom8.wordpress.com or on her YouTube channel at https://www.youtube.com/user/redheadmom8.

BRANDY VENCEL has been homeschooling her four children using Charlotte Mason's philosophy for over a decade. She is co-host of the popular podcast Scholé Sisters and author of *Start Here: A Journey Through Charlotte Mason's 20 Principles*. You can find her blogging about educational philosophy, reading, and homeschool life at Afterthoughts (afterthoughtsblog.net). Brandy and her family live in California with their dog, cat, rabbit menagerie, and a small cage full of praying mantises.

MYSTIE WINCKLER and her husband, Matt, have five children whom they educate classically, seeking to cultivate wisdom and virtue in themselves as well as their children, through discipleship in a simple life full of Truth, Goodness, Beauty—and a lot of books. She helps women transition from stress and chaos to calm clarity at SimplyConvivial.com.

ABOUT THE AUTHOR

PAM BARNHILL believes that you don't have to sacrifice relationships to homeschool strong.

An award-winning educator and former journalist, she has a knack for breaking down big tasks into small, manageable steps and getting to the heart of the stories her listeners want to hear.

Pam is a homeschool speaker, the host of the *Homeschool Solutions Show* podcast, and the author of *Better Together: Simplify Your Homeschool, Strengthen Your Family, and Savor the Subjects That Matter Most*, a book about Morning Time.

Pam lives in the Deep South with her husband, three (mostly) awesome kids, and a passel of family dogs.

Connect with Pam by emailing her at pam@pambarnhill.com or joining her mailing list at pambarnhill.com.